Sports Theology

Playing Inside Out

By: Greg S. Smith, M.Div.,LPC

To Tim
keep up the
good work

Greg Smith can be contacted through www.sportstheology.com or
smith8508@att.net

First published by Dog Ear Publishing
4010 W. 86th Street, Ste H
Indianapolis, IN 46268
www.dogearpublishing.net

dog ear
PUBLISHING

ISBN: 978-160844-338-3

This book is printed on acid-free paper.

Printed in the United States of America

Dedicated to my wife Debbie for her devotion, to Jo, John and Angela for their encouragement and to Christ for his friendship and sacrifice.

Forward

Having spent thirty years in baseball at the professional level as a player and at the Division I level of college baseball as a coach, attempting to unravel the mysteries that beguile athletic performance has been at the core my evaluation process. All of us have seen dozen of cases where players with very similar skill sets perform at vastly different levels. In almost every case of such disparity, the one clear observance is that the high level performer is able to deal with and process anxiety, pressure and stress.

Whether the skill is throwing a baseball, making a putt, or shooting a free throw, the free flowing uninhibited movement pattern wins out every time. But, how do the consistent performers deal with these potential obstacles to success? There have been countless theories and remedial systems utilized by coaches, counselors, and teachers to train individuals for the purpose of minimizing these pressures. Among these have been meditation, focal diversion, and visualization techniques designed to free the mind and allow natural abilities to be free of inhibition.

Therein lies the value of Greg Smith's insightful work Sports Theology – Playing Inside Out. Greg offers a thoughtful introspective that I believe passes the test of psychological plausibility and at the same time provides numerous anecdotal confirmations. Anyone who works with young athletes or others who are struggling to succeed in non-athletic endeavors can benefit from this approach to consistent performance. Many successful people use the techniques described in this book without even knowing it, but for those who may be struggling to achieve, a conscious effort to reach serenity through spiritual perspective can be an effective solution. Over and over we hear star athletes speak of being "in the zone"' to describe outstanding performances. The "zone" to which they are trying to verbalize is a clear minded and stress free centering on the process at hand. Achieving this state of focus is to me what Greg is expounding in this work. I heartily endorse sports theology as an effective learning tool for anyone involved with performance enhancement be it athletic or otherwise.

Hal Baird
Pitcher - Kansas City Royals
Organization 1971-1976
Head Baseball Coach -
Auburn University 1985-2000

Table of Contents

Introduction

Introduction

Sports psychology and sports theology are similar in the sense that they both take established bodies of knowledge and apply them to athletic performance. Sports psychology seeks to understand psychological/mental factors that affect performance in sports, physical activity, and exercise and then attempt to apply these principles to enhance individual and team performance.

Sports theology is based on the premise that God has created us all in his image and with unique gifts. It is his desire that we acknowledge and nurture these gifts. Athletic ability, like all other gifts, can only be fully realized when we are in right relationship with him. Athletic gifts are no different than those of compassion, wisdom, leadership, etc. If we move away from God, or let things get between him and us, we limit his power, which limits our potential.

One of the major differences between sports psychology and sports theology is the starting point. Sports psychology sees athletic excellence coming from what the athlete can learn through concepts like, imagery, motivation and focus. It talks about neural pathways, self-talk and positive thinking. Sports theology believes that athletic excellence comes from utilization of the gifts we have been given, and learning to minimize those things that distract us from meeting our potential. In short, sports theology is not about acquiring skill but rather is about getting out of God's way and letting his gifts shine through.

The principles in sports theology are not unique or applicable only to athletes. Many individuals have to perform at a high level that requires focus, confidence and motivation. The pressure on a CEO can be as intense as it is for the professional athlete. The surgeon certainly needs to be as focused and confident as the PGA golfer. Flight crews are called on to work as a team. We all have things in our lives that mean as much to us as making the winning shot or scoring the winning touchdown.

The major focus of my ministry has always been to communicate to my clients that Christianity should enhance their daily lives. I have found that many individuals genuinely believe in God but have a hard time translating theology into practical daily living. The New Testament is full of promises that insure that God is with us and wants us to live "the abundant life." By not understanding and/or accepting these promises we have relegated ourselves to a nominal life, void of the potential that is available. This "self-limitation" affects all aspects of life, which includes athletic performance

In the following pages we will look at the principles of the Christian faith and how these theological truths enhance athletic excellence. In sports theology (as in any performance), what produces excellence tends to be less important than what prevents it.

CHAPTER 1

Purpose – Perspective

In my observation, many individuals do not understand or believe that Christianity can make an impact in their daily lives. This is the untapped power in the relationship between athletic performance and the Christian faith.

God was intentional in everything he created. In the first chapter of Genesis we are told that he created man "In his own image." Gen 1:31 says, *God saw everything that he had made, and, behold, it was very good.*" We read in Romans 11:36 that everything comes from God alone. Everything lives by his power, and everything is for his glory. Suffice to say, God was purposeful in everything he made.

Rick Warren, in his book *The Purpose Driven Life*, tells us, "Long before you were conceived by your parents, you were conceived in the mind of God. He thought of you first. It is not fate, nor chance, nor luck, nor coincidence that you are breathing at this moment." God specifically made you unique as to race, stature, personality and athletic ability. If God was so intentional about your individual qualities, does it not follow that he has a purpose for his creation? The answer is yes as we read in Romans 8:28, *"And we know that to them that love God all things work together for good, to them that are called according to (his) purpose"* (ASV). When Rick Warren was asked to define his purpose in life he replied, "to prepare for eternity."

Living our lives based on this definition of purpose brings great advantages. First, it gives us a sense of **confidence**. What better source for power than God himself, who has ordained us to perform according to his purpose. True confidence comes when I know that I can rely on the power of God who promises, *"the Lord gives victory to the anointed"* (Psalms 20:6) (NIV). True confidence comes from relying on the fact that God knows what he is doing and I am in tune with him. "Christian confidence" means that with Christ we can handle what-ever life brings. Hebrews 4:16 tells us, "*Let us then approach God's throne of grace with confidence, so that we may receive mercy and find grace to help us in our time of need* (NIV).

As athletes, self-confidence also comes from this relationship with God. They can approach the world with self-confidence because God has equipped them for success. Christian athletes have personal value, not from their own accomplishments, but because God loves them so much that he sacrificed his only Son (John 3:16). We are told in Jeremiah 17:7-8, "*But blessed are those who trust in the LORD, whose confidence is in him. They will be like a tree planted by the water that sends out its roots by the stream. It does not fear when heat comes; its leaves are always green. It has no worries in a year of drought and never fails to bear fruit*" (ASV). This is the basis of athletic self-confidence.

The second advantage of knowing our purpose is that it changes the athlete's view of **preparation**. If we need a ten foot putt to win a tournament or if it takes a free throw to win a game, it helps if we have made a few before. As the champion bull rider says, "This is not my first rodeo." Christian athletes have prepared well because they know what is required and where they are going. In 2 Timothy 4:2 we are told, "*Preach the word; be prepared in season and out of season; correct, rebuke and encourage – with great patience and careful instruc-tion*" (NIV).

We have all heard it said that 90% of athletic excellence is mental. That may sound true but I do not believe most athletes would agree.   If this is true then why do athletes spend so much time in physical preparation? I think it would be safe to say that a professional golfer has spent some time on the range, an Olympic swimmer has spent some time in the pool and the all-pro quarterback has taken a few reps. The point here is that a large part of any athletic success comes from dedicated preparation. How many times have you heard a football player credit the hard off-season workouts for the team's success? I would think that practice accounts for more that 10% of any given athletic outcome. Joe Paterno once said, "To win is important, but the will to prepare is vital."

Most athletes will tell you that there is a lot more time spent in preparation than in actual competition. These same athletes will also tell you that they would rather play than train. Who can blame them? Months or even years before competition, there are endless hours of jumping rope, miles on the treadmill or countless repetitions in the gym, all requiring dedication and perseverance.

No matter if you call it the will to prepare, work ethic or just plain drive; practice is a hard-sell. The premise of this book is that Christianity can help athletic performance. This is especially true when it comes to training or practice. The advantage the Christian athlete has when it comes to the hours of grueling and boring practice is that even this activity glorifies God. Honing one's athletic ability is acknowledging God's gift. Athletic preparation is a combination of good stewardship and celebration of God's gift. Suddenly practice has meaning and purpose of its own.

The Christian athlete knows that practice is more than the development of certain skills needed to perform. Preparation not only trains the body, it also trains the mind. Practice not only builds muscle memory it also provides the athlete with the opportunity to grow in his or her faith. From the Christian point of view practice is about obedience and the building of spiritual character. We are told this in James 1:4, *"Let perseverance finish its work so that you may be mature and complete, not lacking anything"* (NIV). In Romans 5:4, we are told, *" Perseverance, character; and character, hope"* (NIV). The athlete who understands these truths approaches practice with willingness and enthusiasm. Practice then becomes celebration not work.

The third advantage of playing with a sense of God's purpose is that as athletes, we never **compete alone**. God has a vested interest in who we are and the gifts we have been given. PGA player Lee Janzen refers to this when he talks about his win in the US. Open:

> *"So I center myself in Scripture and pray for the things I think God wants. I try to pray for His will, not mine. It's true that there are times — I believe my second U.S. Open victory at the Olympic Club was one of these — when God seems to thrust His hand right into the middle of my golf game."*

We have all heard the saying that, " God is my co-pilot." For the Christian athlete, there is confidence in knowing that God is 'on my bag', in my corner or on my team.

The fourth thing purposeful living does, is it gives our life ***meaning***. We are "called to glorify God." We see this demonstrated in the life of Christ. In John 8:24 Jesus says, *"If I glorify myself, my glory means nothing. My Father, whom you claim as your God, is the one who glorifies me"* (NIV). Even facing His crucifixion, Jesus never lost this sense of purpose. We see this in John 17:1, which reads, "... *and lifting up his eyes to heaven, he said, Father, the hour is come; glorify thy Son, that the son may glorify thee"* (ASV). Once again our gifts are not given to glorify ourselves but rather to glorify God.

We are specifically made and specifically called. God has a place for us in his plan and has provided us with unique gifts to accomplish the spiritual tasks at hand. We are called to serve him and share the Gospel with others. Matthew tells us, *"In the same way, let your light shine before others, that they may see your good deeds and glorify your Father in heaven"* (Matthew 5:16)(ASV). Likewise, we are told in 2 Corinthians 9:13, " *Because of the service by which you have proved yourselves, people will praise God for the obedience that accompanies your confession of the gospel of Christ, and for your generosity in sharing with them and with everyone else"* (ASV).

In James 1:2-3, James tells us, *"Consider all things pure joy, my brothers, whenever you face trials of many kinds, because you know that the testing of your faith develops perseverance"* (NIV). James can say this because he sees everything that happens as an opportunity to glorify God. James is able to find meaning in whatever happens. Knowing that we can glorify God in

9

every situation gives us direction and brings meaning to all aspects of our lives. Plainly stated, God loves us and we have work to do!

Orel Hershiser, National League Cy Young award winner, once said, "You give your best, you do the ultimate and then you give praise where the ability came from, and the ability came from God." This is the meaning of athletic performance for the Christian athlete. As a Christian it does not matter what comes our way or what happens; we can accomplish the purpose for which we were made—we can always glorify God.

In the arena of professional sports life can easily lose its meaning. It is tough dealing with the constant pressure to perform, the physical toll placed on the body and the stress that comes with a high-profile life. It is easy to begin to question what it is all for. The Christian athlete never has to ask this question. For this athlete the answer is simple, use God's gifts to glorify Him. Athletic performance then becomes two dimensional, one being the competition itself and the other being ministry.

Personal satisfaction for the theologically-based athlete not only comes from performing well but also from sharing the Gospel through this performance. There is great satisfaction in doing what we were made to do and understanding why we do it. David Robinson, formerly of the San Antonio Spurs, was quoted to say, "I want the fans to see and know Jesus. I want my teammates to see and know Jesus." This is an example of an athlete who knows the meaning of athletic performance.

Lastly, knowing God's purpose for our lives broadens our *perspective*. To live our lives with a sense of God's purpose means living our lives spiritually. Living spiritually frees us from being caught up in the distractions of this world. We are warned about living our lives in this world in 1 John 2:15, *"Do not love the world or anything in the world. If you love the world, love for the Father is not in you"* (ASV). Conversely, we are promised that through Christ we can live above the world as seen in John 16: 33, *"I have told you these things, so that in me you may have peace. In this world you will have trouble. But take heart! I have overcome the world"* (ASV).

Spiritual living allows us to see the world and the events in the world from God's vantage point. Living on the promises of Christ enables us to prioritize and make decisions based on our faith instead of our flesh. Remaining "Christ centered" is not easy and is a battle we as Christians must continually fight. This conflict is referenced in Ephesians 6:12, *"For we are not fighting against flesh-and-blood enemies, but against evil rulers and authorities of the unseen world, against mighty powers in this dark world, and against evil spirits in the heavenly places"* (NLT).

If we try to fight these spiritual battles alone we will fall prey to the world and its temptations. Without Christ at our side we will spend much of our time and life fighting daily battles that skew our perspective — battles we cannot win without him. By living purposefully and spiritually we are not distracted and are never alone. Through Christ we are transformed, we are a new creation, which is referred to in Psalms 51:10, *"Create in me a clean heart (spirit), oh Lord, and renew a right mind within me"* (ASV). As Christians we maintain our perspective by relying on the truth found in John 14:17, "*The Spirit of truth. The world cannot accept him, because it neither sees him nor knows him. But you know him, for he lives with you and will be in you*" (ASV).

The ability to see things from God's perspective allows us to not only live above the distractions of the world; it allows us to see past the moment. It allows us to approach every situation with the knowledge that "this too shall pass." Because we have confidence, have been specifically called and have a Godly perspective, great things are possible.

We have addressed how a theological perspective helps athletes prepare, perform with confidence and find meaning in what they do. The payoff for athletes who have a spiritual view or perspective relates to overcoming pressure and stress in performance. Knowing that no matter what happens on the field of play, athletes are free to meet their real goals and purpose. It helps take the pressure off of any competition, and therefore, increases the opportunity for excellence. They perform with joy and enthusiasm — which is how games are to be played.

Granted, there are some differences in the pressures of the athlete. This is especially true for athletes who perform at the highest level. Most of us do not perform our jobs on national television or in front of thousands. Very few of us prepare for years for one event or one moment that brings instant success or failure. Our daily performance is not replayed on ESPN or streamed across the Internet on YouTube. Realistically speaking there is pressure and then there is pressure!

In my opinion nothing helps the athlete relieve this pressure more than knowing that God has made him or her on purpose for a purpose. Knowing that personal athletic gifts are from God, and that he wants these gifts used to glorify him, makes all the difference. As Babe Ruth once said, "God had an eye out for me, just as he has for you, and he was pulling for me to make the grade." The ramifications of this truth can profoundly impact athletic performance.

Kendall Simmons, eight-year veteran with the Pittsburgh Steelers, told me that when it came to performance, his first year was his best. He attributes this to the fact that in his first year he played with joy and pure love for the game. He told me, "I was having fun, and I was a kid playing the game I had always loved to play."

Michelle Akers, Women's Soccer Player of the Century, puts it this way, "The more time I spend keeping my eye on who God is, his perspective, his goal for me, the more fun I have, the more joyful I feel, the more peace I have." This is the essence of the spiritual athletic experience, playing for God and having fun doing it.

Christian athletes who understand their place in God's heart always win. No matter if it is practicing or performing, these athletes know that there is no losing in following Christ. No matter what is ahead of them, God is behind them, " *Beloved, I pray that you may prosper in all things and be in health, just as your soul prospers*" (3 John 1:2) (NKJV). PGA player Loren Roberts puts it best when he says, "God wants you to try your best. He wants you to give him the glory for your achievements. So obviously, he wants you to win."

Athletes who understand God's purpose for their lives perform with meaning. In reference to preparation, confidence or pressure, God's perspective allows the

Christian athlete to never compete alone and to always win. This is a good description of what it is like to perform in concert with God's purpose and from his perspective.

CHAPTER 2

Sin-Distraction

Theologically speaking, whatever causes us to become separated from God is called sin. In sports theology, those things that hinder our athletic gifts are called distractions.

Christianity is not complicated. God created us in his image, we moved away from him and he sacrificed his son to guarantee our return. The Christian life is an easy life. No, it really is. We just have to accept Christ, be forgiven, and live the spirit-filled life. Theologically we can go around the block four or five times but we will still end up where we started — relying on a simple faith. The Christian life should be easy but it does not always seem that way.

Why is it that we have made the Christian experience so difficult? Is it God, has he changed the plan or the rules, has he thrown us some curves to confuse us? The answer is a resounding no! God remains constant which is the only thing we know for sure (Hebrews 13:9). The reason we struggle spiritually is because we have moved away from him. Our original state was one of perfection. We are told this is Genesis 1:27-28,

> *"God created man in his own image, in the image of God created he him; male and female created he them. And God blessed them: and God said unto them, Be fruitful, and multiply, and replenish the earth, and subdue it; and have dominion over the fish of the sea, and over the birds of the heavens, and over every living thing that moveth upon the earth" (ASV).*

This original relationship between God and man was changed forever by Adam's choice to break this

covenant. Adam's eating from the tree "in the midst of
the Garden" (the only limitation put on man by God) put
man's will at odds with the will of God. The nature of
man changed. This is described in Genesis 3:7-8, which
says,

> "And the eyes of them both were opened,
> and they knew that they were naked; and
> they sewed fig-leaves together, and made
> themselves aprons. And they heard the
> voice of Jehovah God walking in the gar-
> den in the cool of the day: and the man
> and his wife hid themselves from the pres-
> ence of Jehovah God amongst the trees of
> the garden" (ASV).

Man would now have to work to regain the relationship
with God that he once had. Adam had introduced sin into
a perfect world.

We are sinners. The acknowledgement of our sin
is the first step in our return to God. We are sinners and
that is the state in which we now live. We can rationalize that we are good and convince ourselves that we are
in God's will, but the fact is that we are "yet sinners."
The salvation process is confession, forgiveness and then
sanctification. Confession of our sins is key. Confession tells God that we understand that we have "fallen
short of the glory of God" and need his forgiveness.
Confession is our response to God and movement toward
him. Moving toward God is what he desires and what
was missing with Adam. Without owning our sins we
cannot confess them. Without confession we cannot

receive forgiveness for those sins. Without confession and forgiveness we limit the ability to change our sinful behavior.

Martin Luther once said, "Love God and sin boldly." What this statement means to me is that we should not live our lives out of fear of sinning, for we will always sin. We should live our lives under the love and grace of a God who loves us in spite of our sin. "Sin boldly" means to me that we should not try to rationalize or cover up our sins, but rather we should recognize them, own them, and confess them "boldly" to God.

The problem is not that God is surprised or devastated by our sin; he knows the sinful nature of man. The real problem is our inability to accept ourselves as sinners. I am not saying that it is all right to sin or to sin without regret. I am saying that we need not let our propensity to sin separate us from our Lord. We live under a different covenant than Adam and Eve lived. Their sin and expulsion set them on a hard path. The expulsion from the Garden and God's command to "work the ground from which he was taken" (Genesis 3:23) was man's only way to repair the damage that had been done. We, on the other hand, are post-Christ; we are resurrected people, justified by the blood of Jesus.

We cannot change the fact that Adam sinned but we can react differently to our own. If our response to sin is to, hide or run from his presence, then we have learned nothing from Adam. We have learned nothing from the sacrifice or teachings of Christ.

Sports theology works on the premise that God has given us gifts and he wants us to maximize these gifts to glorify him. The only thing that limits the potential of these gifts is our inability to focus on God and his purpose for us. Theologically speaking, whatever causes us to become separated from God is called sin. In sports theology, those things that hinder our athletic gifts are called distractions. No matter if you call it sin or distraction, it can limit our (gifts) performance. It goes without saying that athletes who perform at the highest levels have plenty of potential distractions.

What was Adam's first sin? Some say it was *pride*. Pride, like many words in the English language can be positive or negative depending on the context in which it is used. We see this as we look at Webster's definition of pride. The first definition is, *the quality or state of being proud: as a: inordinate self-esteem: conceit*. The second primary meaning of pride is, *a reasonable or justifiable self-respect.* Although these meanings appear to be similar, they are vastly difference when lived out.

When I talk about the pitfalls of living out of pride I am referring to the former definition not the latter. In Mark 7:22-23 we see that this definition of pride has made the list of "inner things" that defile mankind, " … adultery, greed, wickedness, deceit, lustful desires, envy, slander, pride, and foolishness. All these vile things come from within; they are what defile you"(NLT). Ted Simmons, a 20-year veteran in the Major Leagues and eight-time All-star, once said, "There are things about some professional athletes that I cannot stand — the pretense, the egos, the pomposity, the greed." The most familiar passage in the Bible about pride is found in Proverbs 16:18, "Pride goes before destruction, and haughtiness before a fall"(NLT).

Carl Jung, a renowned psychologist, once said this in reference to the first meaning of pride, "Through pride we are ever deceiving ourselves. But deep down below the surface of the average conscience a still, small voice says to us, 'something is out of tune'." Pride (conceit) attempts to make us more than we are and tells us we are better than others. There is a significant difference in claiming personal credit for what I have accomplished and giving God the glory for the gifts I have been given. It is bad enough to let our accomplishments "go to our heads", it is even worse to let our accomplishments "go to our hearts."

Pride is a slippery slope. If athletes begin to take sole credit for their success then they are on their own and have separated themselves from God. This not only limits God's ability to maximize their athletic gifts, it puts tremendous pressure on their shoulders. It is a slippery slope because eventually these athletes tie their value to performance or success and must constantly work to stay on top. This is the pressure that many athletes feel and succumb to. This is why you hear many Christian athletes talk about the freedom they feel when the credit and glory of performance is given to God. Kim Anthony, world-class gymnast speaks to this as she says,

> *"...my life and attitude have changed. No longer do I look to the opinions of others, or my own accomplishments to give me value. Now I look to the unconditional love of God, knowing that He created me as an unique individual with a very special purpose."*

Pride not only pits our will against the will of God (Adam's issue), it pits the athlete against everyone else. Some would say that this is the point of competition in the first place. I see their point, but pride has the tendency to linger long after competition ends. Individuals and athletes who are fueled by pride (conceit) become full of themselves. This condition negatively affects all aspects of life, which include friendships, marriage and the ability to be a team player.

The aloof lifestyle of pride creates a life of isolation. Prideful athletes find themselves alone or only surrounded by people who want something from them. The pressure that comes from depending on "self" to perform and the feelings brought on by isolation will eventually hinder performance. In essence, pride seduces the athlete into valuing something that it eventually destroys—excellence in performance.

In the defense of the professional athlete, it is hard not to feel superior or to get "puffed up." Our culture tends to worship them. They are paid large sums of money, constantly pursued by fans, the press and everything else that comes with being a celebrity. It is difficult to be humble in that environment. It must be hard to keep things in perspective. It would be easy to be seduced by the world and begin to believe that true value comes from material things: to fall into the trap of replacing God with oneself.

The Christian athlete is able to keep things in perspective by relying on God rather than the things the world has to offer. Jesus fought this battle when Satan tempted him in in the desert. We see how Jesus dealt with the temptation of worldly rewards in Matthew 4:8-10,

> *"Again, the devil took him to a very high mountain and showed him all the kingdoms of the world and their splendor. 'All this I will give you,' he said, 'if you will bow down and worship me'. Jesus said to him, 'Away from me, Satan! For it is written: Worship the Lord your God, and serve him only'" (NIV).*

Jesus was able to deny Satan and keep his perspective because he knew where he had come from and where he was going. Jesus' strength to reject the temptations of the world came not from his own power (pride) but from knowing God's purpose for him. Christian athletes handle the distractions and temptations of the world the same way—by relying on God, not themselves.

Jennifer Azzi, of the Utah Stars, knows what it is like to perform with a sense of God's purpose when she says,

> *"The strength God gives me is an area where my faith has become more evident. Now, if things aren't going my way, I tend to look at it from God's point of view instead of my point of view. That frees me up from worrying so much about my performance or myself. I think it is just human nature that your thoughts get negative or your thoughts tend to revolve*

*more around yourself. My faith has really
freed me up from all that. I asked Jesus to
enter my life and make me the person He
wanted me to be."*

Christian athletes are free to perform without the
distractions brought on by pride. Their will is not at odds
with God's will and they can perform at the level God
has equipped them to perform.

While some think what makes us sin is pride,
others believe it is *fear*. Webster's definition of fear, as
it is used today, means *dread, alarm, and feelings of
uneasiness*. It is clear to me that Adam's response to
hide from God was based on the fear of what God would
do. There is always a connection between lack of trust
and fear when it comes to relationships. Adam's reaction
makes sense when you consider that he did not trust God
to know what was best for him in the first place. Adam
obviously made the same mistake we do, expecting God
to do what we would do.

As a counselor, I always tell my clients that I
believe the opposite of love is fear — not hate. I base
this belief on the words of the Apostle John who tells us
in 1 John 4:18-19, *"There is no fear in love. But perfect
love drives out fear, because fear has to do with punishment. The one who fears is not made perfect in love. We
love because he first loved us"* (NIV). In relationships,
fear usually comes from not trusting others, fearing that
others will hurt us. *True love* is based on trust and faith
in another—the way God loves us.

If Adam and Eve did hide from God out of fear
(dread), then they either did not understand God's char-

acter or did not trust it. It is important to point out that Adam and Eve only felt fear after they sinned. This sequence tells me that fear is not part of the perfect relationship that God had intended. The same can be said for us if we tend to fear God. In other words, fear is an emotional condition that man first felt in response to his disobedience. If Adam had obeyed God we, would not be discussing fear, as we know it. Fearing (dreading) God is basically evaluating his character through the eyes of man, which puts God on our level. Once again, *perfect love* is from God; fear is not.

I find myself telling clients all the time that they cannot find peace in life if they live out of fear. Franklin D. Roosevelt was right when he said, "all we have to fear is fear itself." Fear has the tendency to "freeze us". It prevents us from doing what we need to do and being who we need to be. As Christians we cannot move God's kingdom forward or fulfill the great commission if we are afraid to *do*. We are not going to be a good friend, a good neighbor, or a good spouse or a good athlete if we live out of fear. The spirit-filled life can only be achieved when we are free of such feelings of anxiety and dread. This is the power of the Psalms 23.

Fear is primal, which means it is basic to the human condition. Primal fear is a survival mechanism used to protect early man from a hostile environment. It is the basis of the "fight or flight" syndrome, which is an involuntary physiological reaction to a threat. This fight or flight response sends blood to big muscles, raises the heart rate, increases adrenalin levels, etc. This survival reaction is to be used in short bursts to defend oneself or to flee an immediate threat.

Fear in this context is not necessarily bad (you can even see how this fight or flight reaction could be an advantage for the athlete). The problem comes when an individual views everything as a threat and functions in a constant or prolonged state of fight or flight. These individuals cannot determine real threats from false threats. Remaining in this "alert state" causes mental and physical fatigue and eventually distracts from performance. When I talk about fear as being a distraction to performance I am talking about living in constant fear, not this physiological response to a real threat.

As a therapist I see a lot of people who live in fear. In my experience, fear of failure and the fear of rejection are the most prevalent. Each one of these fears can be powerful alone but when combined, they can be devastating. Sure, no one likes to fail, but if failure means I am not valuable as a person, then it is a whole other matter. If an athlete ties his or her self-worth to performance, then failure *is* to be feared and becomes debilitating. I asked Kendall Simmons, eight-year starting offensive lineman for the Pittsburgh Steelers, if he felt he could play in the NFL and be afraid. He told me, "No way! Fear makes you a step slower, second guess your assignment, and play on your heels, all of which will get you hammered and the quarterback killed."

Athletes who allow their performance to "mean everything" are setting themselves up to perform out of fear. Christian athletes, on the other hand, know that their value does not come from performance. They know that God loves them unconditionally and that their value is demonstrated by the sacrifice of Christ on their behalf. They perform to glorify their value, not earn it. Tom

Lehman, 19-year PGA player and winner of the 1996 British Open says it this way,

> *"Winning the British Open was a thrill of a lifetime. But I learned a long time ago that the thrill of victory is fleeting. It's not long before you find yourself asking, what's next? As much as I longed to win a major championship, it didn't change anything. I was still the same person as before. I had the same hang-ups, the same problems—and even some new ones. The Bible says, "All men are like grass and their glory is like the flowers of the field. The grass withers and the flowers fall. So what is it that lasts? The only thing that has given my life true meaning—my relationship with Jesus Christ."*

There are other fears for the professional athlete. There is the fear of being cut, getting hurt, being benched, letting the team down, etc. (and these are just the fears that surround his or her sport). To perform well at the highest level, the athlete must avoid the distraction of these fears as well. Brent Jones, of the San Francisco 49ers speaks to this,

> *"The Lord has also given me the strength and courage to deal with career threatening injuries, and it's only by His grace that I have been able to continue to perform. 'My grace is sufficient for you, for*

my power is made perfect in weakness' (2 Corinthians 12:9). Until I turned my life over to Jesus Christ, I never had real joy, peace and contentment on the inside."

Lou Brock once said, "Show me a guy who's afraid to look bad, and I'll show you a guy you can beat every time." Babe Ruth was quoted to say, "Don't let the fear of striking out hold you back." When it came to fear, Napoleon said, "He who fears being conquered is sure of defeat." According to these guys, when it comes to performance, fear is the ultimate distraction. This is the fear that Kendall Simmons says has no place on the football field.

The Christian athlete does not perform out of fear but rather out of confidence (courage) that comes from Proverbs 29:25, *"The fear of man is a trap, but whoever leans on, trusts in, and puts his confidence in the Lord is safe and set on high"*(AMP). Athletes, who perform theologically, compete with confidence, courage and assurance. They perform knowing that God has given them all they need, "Fear not, little flock; for it is your Father's good pleasure to give you the kingdom" (Luke 12:32) (ASV). The Christian athlete avoids the distraction of fear because he or she cannot fail.

Although pride and fear are good reasons why Adam may have sinned, the need for *control* is also worth mentioning. Control is the temptation and curse of fallen man. For whatever reason, Adam was not willing to rely on God and wanted to be more: to be equal and to control his own life. The need to be in control immediately puts us in the center of our own belief system, with everything revolving around us. This attempt to take control is why God had to do something. Adam had created another God, so to speak, himself.

Issues involving control are difficult to identify because we tend to rationalize that we are just "being responsible" or that we just "like to have things in order." We tell ourselves that we are just taking charge of our lives and want to be thorough, and if this means taking charge of those around us, then so be it.

In reality, control is self-serving and has no benefit to others. It is denial to call control *leadership* or *ambition*. I am not talking about personalities that like to meet a schedule or want to be prepared in their daily lives. I am talking about those people who are at the center of their own world. Control is all about *them*. They think that being in control somehow protects them from the trials and tribulations of this world. They of course are mistaken. Needing control to be happy does not work for two reasons. First, it is impossible to be in total control, a fact that haunts this individual. Secondly, control ends up separating the individual from those around them, which causes isolation, bitterness and depression. Most importantly, control separates us from God.

Ironically, control sets up the exact situation that we feared in the first place. By separating ourselves from God through our need for control, we limit those things that we need the most: love, acceptance and nurturing. Whatever Adam thought he needed or was afraid he did not have, his movement away from God brought him further loneliness, shame and fear. The constant prayer for the control freak should be: "Let go and let God."

As we have mentioned, Adam chose control over faith. This is important to remember for two reasons. First, it reminds us that the desire for control is part of the nature of man, and second, Adam became lost when he got it. The interaction between control and faith has always interested me. No matter if you are talking about control and faith theologically or psychologically, they tend to be at odds with one another. The more one increases the more the other decreases.

I have always said that in any sport where a ball or a referee is involved, control is out the window. If we are only comfortable in life when we have control then we are either constantly uneasy or in denial. In this world anything can happen. This is especially true in sports. You do not have to tell Greg Norman this. In 1986 Bob Tway holes a sand shot (which appeared to be on the way out of bounds) to beat Norman by 2 strokes in the PGA Championship. One year later Larry Mize holes a 140-foot chip shot to beat Norman in the Masters. In 1990, at the Bay Hill Invitational, Robert Gamez holes-out from the fairway on the 18th hole to beat Norman by one.

The need for control is the problem with the "prevent defense" (affectionately called "prevent win") in football. How many times have we seen one team dominate a game and then loose in the final minute playing to control the outcome? I have always thought that they lost faith just before they lost the game. When the game or match is on the line you cannot start trying to aim (control) tee shots in golf or a serve in tennis. Control is born out of doubt and mistrust in one's ability and inevitably distracts from performance.

The athlete who performs theologically is not concerned about the things he or she cannot control. They are not superstitious. They do not wear the same socks, eat the same meal or listen to the same music before each game for luck. They are free to focus on the task at hand because they know that God is in control. Christian athletes know that no matter what happens on the field of play or in life, that God has a purpose and they have an opportunity to glorify Him. Shaun Alexander, of the Seattle Seahawks, says it best, "It can be the stormiest day in the world, but I don't worry about it. I know God is going to take care of me."

Pride, fear, and control are all decent arguments for why Adam disobeyed God, but for me, the answer has always been "*unfaith*." You may not find this word in the dictionary, but it sure has meaning in life. No matter what Adam felt or thought, he was not faithful. He obviously did not trust God. Now we can haggle over the difference between trust and faith, but we would not gain much. Let us just say that faith refers to the belief that God is sovereign and through this statement of faith, we find salvation.

Trust, on the other hand, usually relates to confidence in something that can be seen or touched. While trust refers to a cognitive affirmation in something that we can deduce to be valid or true, faith, means having confidence in something that is beyond proof or is incomprehensible. Jesus refers to this definition of faith when he tells Thomas, "*Blessed are those who believe and have not seen*" (John 20:29) (ASV). In either case Adam did not believe that God's way was his way. Adam pursued a direction that we all tend to pursue, his own.

Could it be as simple as "we are saved by grace *through faith*" so therefore we were separated from God by unfaith? Doubt and mistrust can undermine our relationship with God. Faith is powerful and if it is this faith that brings us to Christ then we need to guard it, nourish it and use it.

1 Corinthians 15:45 tells us, *"The first man, Adam, became a living person. But the last Adam—that is, Christ—is a life-giving Spirit"* (NLT). In Jesus we see who man originally was and who we can be again. Granted, Jesus demonstrated (and continues to demonstrate) God's love for us, and God's willingness to sacrifice for our salvation, but Jesus also showed (and continues to show) us what living our lives in the image of God is like. Our attempt to be Christ-like is to pursue our original place; in fact, it is our only way back (2 Corinthians 4:4).

Thus, we have the two natures of man: one that innately wants to move toward God and one that, due to the fall, moves away from God. This is the daily battle that we fight as Christians, *"...and be found in him, not having a righteousness of mine own, (even) that which is of the law, but that which is through faith in Christ, the righteousness that is from God by faith"* (Philippians 3:9) (ASV). As Christians, our goal is not about perfection but rather the constant desire and pursuit of "knowing Christ" (Philippians 3:10-14).

Faith-based athletes are not devastated by a bad call or bad bounce. They know that not matter what happens in daily life, that God is not shaken and neither is their relationship with him. They live and perform knowing that they have the opportunity to prove their love for God in all situations. Christian athletes know that win, lose or draw they always have the opportunity to move toward him.

Sports theology believes that athletic ability is a gift, like all other gifts, which are given by God to glorify him. In sports theology sin can be described as anything that distracts us from God and his plan for our lives. Pride, fear, and control are distractions that not only diminish or relationship with God; they hinder the use of our gifts and are a detriment to athletic performance. It is through faith that we become all we can be and perform to the best of our ability.

CHAPTER 3
Justification – Motivation

The difference between being motivated to perform and being driven to perform is significant. Christian athletes choose to perform to glorify God; they are not forced (driven) to perform.

Christianity is unique because of its teaching of justification by *grace* (Romans 3:24). The definition of justification is God's saying to us that the demands of his law have been fulfilled in the righteousness of his Son. Justification, then, is based on the work of Christ, accomplished through his blood (Romans 5:9) and brought to his people through his resurrection (Romans 4:25). God is "just" because his holy standard of perfect righteousness is <u>freely</u> available to the believer (Rom 3: 26; 5:16). We are set free.

Although Christ has paid the price for our justification, it is through our faith that he is received and his righteousness is experienced and enjoyed (Romans 3: 24-26). Grace and faith are the two elements of the relationship: grace from God and faith from man. As in any relationship, both conditions are important for the relationship to flourish. If two people do not trust one another or do not believe that each is loved, then the relationship will cease to grow. To avoid this problem God constantly tells us to strengthen our faith; a weak faith creates a weak relationship.

The New Testament sometimes speaks of justification by works. For example, Paul in Romans 2:13 says, "*the doers of the law will be justified*" while James concludes, (James 2:4) "*a man is justified by works, and not by faith alone.*" This thought may seem to be a contradiction to Paul's other statements, "*By deeds of the law no flesh will be justified in his sight* (Romans 3:20) (ASV) or "*That the attempt to be justified through law is equivalent to being 'estranged from Christ' and 'fallen from grace'*" (Galatians 5:4) (ASV).

This statement is not a contradiction because there is a difference between the works of the flesh and the fruits of the Spirit. Works that once were performed in an attempt to appease God are now done as a result of the Holy Spirit in us (Romans 8:1-4). It is important to understand that the law of the Old Testament convicts us and demonstrates our inability to earn our own salvation, "we have been weighed and found wanting". The difference here is between the works of man versus works of faith through Christ (Ephesians 2:15-16). Matthew 5:17 speaks to the real meaning of works and the law. It is here that Jesus tells us that he came, " *not to destroy the law but rather to fulfill it*". Only through Christ can the law be fulfilled. The true order of events in justification is first, grace, second, faith and third, works or in other words, "by grace through faith resulting in works" (Ephesians 2:8).

For us to live theologically we must understand justification. After we accept the fact that we are sinners (the fallen nature of man) and confess our sins, we must then claim God's forgiveness. Without justification there can be neither reconciliation nor a spirit-filled life. Christians who do not understand or claim their justification through Christ's sacrifice will be limited in their ability to live spiritually.

Many Christians struggle with the concept of justification because they are uncomfortable with grace. The fact is, that many times, it is hard to fathom that God has freely forgiven us. Once again the trouble starts when we try to understand God through our own human experiences instead of believing what God has told us. Let me give you an example of how this plays out.

One of the characteristics of fallen man is that of self-centeredness. What this means is that we have the tendency to view everything from our point of view; things are good or bad depending on how we see them. Angry people always feel victimized, jealous people are always envious and insecure people are always in tune with their weaknesses. The point, if we cannot accept God's grace, then we are unable to treat others gracefully. If we do not feel accepted ourselves, then we have a hard time accepting others. It is through God's grace that we live our lives with power and confidence (Acts 20:32). Only when we accept and feel God's unconditional love, can we start serving others and stop focusing only on ourselves (Acts 6:8).

For us to accept God's grace, we must believe a couple of things. First we must believe God when he tells us that we are forgiven and deemed worthy (Colossians 2:13-14). The second thing we must believe is that we are unconditionally loved; in other words, there is nothing we can do to deserve this love (Romans 5: 8-9). We cannot earn God's love; we can only accept it.

The major difference between sports theology, and any other discipline that attempts to improve performance, is motivation. The difference between being **motivated** to perform and being **driven** to perform is significant. In 1991 I was the administrator of a psychiatric hospital that went bankrupt. I was out of work and had been looking for employment for six months. Things were getting pretty difficult financially and I was becoming desperate. I was asked to interview for a position as regional director of a chain of psychiatric hospitals. The money was great and this would be the answer to my financial problems.

During my interview it became obvious that the main concern for this company was the bottom line not quality of care for patients. I was told that my job would be to push administrators to "fill beds" and make their "numbers". I was told that the person for this job needed to be "driven" and was asked if I was this type of person. I remember thinking that cattle are driven to slaughter and dogs drive deer to the hunters. My answer to their question was, " I am *motivated* to help others, but I am certainly not *driven* by money". I did not get the job.

Christian athletes are motivated to glorify God through performance; they are not forced (driven) to perform. Driven athletes, like all driven individuals, begin to feel chased and out of control. These athletes cannot stop or rest until their goals are met, goals that often times, are undefined and/or not even theirs in the first place. Theses athletes are performing out of works not grace.

For the Athlete to perform theologically he or she must understand justification. Being justified in Christ allows Christian athletes to perform freely (grace) based on God's gifts. They do not perform to earn (works) their value. The difference between performing out of grace and works is subtle yet significant. The big difference has to do with pressure the athlete feels. The non-Christian athlete has a lot riding on his or her performance. They are competing for their sense of worth. The Christian athlete already has won this battle and is free to "play the game". Rick Aguilera, 16-year reliever in the Majors, talks about playing out of grace when he says, "This is a free gift God offers to each of us, but we must accept that gift individually. Don't trust in your own good works to earn a ticket to heaven. It is by Christ and him alone that you can be saved."

Justification is the basis of the Christian's **self-esteem**. As a therapist, I am often asked what is the leading reason people come for counseling. For me, the answer is easy: poor self-esteem. Individuals that suffer from a poor self-concept live a difficult life. These people often make poor decisions, tend to capitulate in relationships, and are often victimized in the workplace. They are plagued with a negative view of the world.

The difficult thing about poor-self esteem is it is easily masked; it can be misdiagnosed as anxiety, personality disorders, depression, and so on. Once a person gives up on himself or herself, the world closes in. One of the most difficult things to do is to help a person change, or significantly increase, his/her sense of value or self-worth. One thing is for sure; this negative self-image does not lend itself to living theologically.

Those individuals who feel inferior are always trying to be validated by others. Their self-worth rests on the interactions of others instead of themselves. This need, as you can imagine, creates anxiety and affects their interactions and relationships. Each day they enter the world with the question of self-worth up for grabs. They go through life hoping someone or some thing will make them feel valuable. This quest is most often unsuccessful, which in turn reinforces their original poor self-concept.

Christians living under the justification of Christ do not have to struggle with low self-esteem; they are living theologically (spiritually). A paraphrase of Romans 8:31 says, *"If God likes us who cares what others think."* In other words, who else do we need to impress? It certainly doesn't work the other way around; please everyone else but do not care what God thinks. The Christian who struggles with poor self-esteem, therefore, needs to study justification. Justification means that God's law has been fulfilled. Through Christ, God has reconciled the world to *himself.*

I have always said that "low self-esteem Christian" is a contradiction of terms. How can we feel bad about something God created, and then on our behalf, sacrificed his Son? This is the foundation of justification, *"God so loved the world that he gave his only begotten Son, that whosoever believes in him should not perish but have everlasting life"* (John 3:16) (ASV). This is the basis of self-confidence for the Christian athlete.

In my view, low self-esteem is one of the biggest distractions to excellence in performance. I spoke to the local Section of the PGA and told them that the only tool that athletes consistently bring to any competition is themselves. The latest equipment or technology will not hide an insecure athlete. As we mentioned earlier, low self-esteem individuals tend to expect the worst, make poor decisions and give up — all of which work against performance. It is enough to ask athletes to compete against another without fighting the "demons" within themselves.

This relates to what sports psychology calls visualization. The goal for the athlete is to visualize a particular shot or skill and then produce it in reality. This is difficult for the low self-esteem athlete to do because he or she usually sees things as negative or deals in a world of "worst possible scenarios."

I am presently working with a high school golfer who struggles with a low self-esteem. She has the athletic skills to perform well, but her scores do not reflect her ability. When asked why she plays poorly in competition, she told me that she always has two or three bad holes in the middle of the round. As she explained, even though she always starts well she begins to wonder when things will fall apart. Unfortunately for her, this is not just a thought process that happens on the golf course, it is how she views life. It will be difficult to change her view of performance without addressing the expectations of failure brought on by her low self-esteem.

Christian athletes do not have to fight this individual battle of self-worth. Instead of being haunted by the negative thoughts of the low self-esteem person, they are focused on what is possible in Christ. They see performance as being full of possibilities rather than limitations; glorifying Christ in the performance itself fulfills them.

Another problem that arises when justification is not realized relates to **forgiveness.** If we are not able to claim our own forgiveness then we will have trouble forgiving others. This inability comes into play for a lot of people each day. As a clinician, I can tell you that one of the greatest causes of emotional illness is this inability to negotiate a painful past.

I cannot begin to guess the number of hours therapists spend trying to help people emotionally deal with an abusive relationship, an alcoholic parent or a broken heart that occurred in years past. These clients seem to be unable to move on. As therapists we are taught to talk about "letting go" or helping the client to "achieve closure." Clients tell us that they just cannot seem "to forget" what has happened. The Christian has an advantage when it comes to dealing with the past; he or she can talk about forgiveness not forgetting. Forgiveness has been modeled for the Christian. God forgives us and forgets (neglects) our sinful past, looking forward to our salvation. By using this model of forgiveness, we forgive others because God first forgave us.

Justification also helps us **forgive ourselves**. For many Christians, the struggle is not with forgiving others but rather the inability to "forgive self". These individuals struggle with guilt. We can talk about appropriate and inappropriate guilt and make this difficult, but the fact is that our choice to carry this guilt is just that, our choice.

Guilt in itself is not a bad thing because it many times motivates us to change and/or make restitution to those we have hurt. Holding on to guilt and using it to punish is where the problem lies. Those of us who live with constant guilt either have not confessed our sins or do not believe in God's ability to forgive. Guilt then becomes the basis for a deeper problem, which negatively affects our relationship with God. A process we saw play out with Adam in the garden.

One of the most important things for an athlete to do is to put bad luck, bad plays or a bad performance in the past. It has been said, " One of the best skills an athlete can possess is a short memory". In most sports, things happen in a split second and the athlete needs to be able to focus on the next play, event or skill and not be wrapped up in what just happened. Athletes at the highest level tend to be hardest on themselves. They have high standards and expectations when it comes to their performance.

These athletes need to avoid getting down on themselves and learn to accept the bad with the good. When it comes to their own performance they need to learn to forgive themselves and then forget. All the coaxing or coaching in the world does not comfort athletes who are overly hard on themselves. How many times have you heard a team member tell a player, "don't get down on yourself," to no avail? This reassurance from another does not help the athlete who struggles with self-forgiveness because the pressure to succeed and personal disdain is internal.

Theologically-based athletes understand the dynamic of forgiveness through justification, which is modeled for them through the sacrifice of Christ. For them, it does not make much sense to be hard on themselves for a particular performance when God himself can forgive them for sin. The Christian athlete is free to perform knowing that he/she is fallible and mistakes will be made. They are able to let go of past events knowing that character and faith grow from adversity not in preventing it.

I recall what Roy McAvoy (Kevin Costner) says about the golf swing in the movie <u>Tin Cup</u>, "*Pulled into position not by the hands, but by the body which turns away from the target shifting weight to the right side without shifting balance. Tempo is everything; perfection unobtainable...*" For Christian athletes "unobtainable perfection" is manageable because they are perfected in Christ.

Perhaps the biggest downside in not accepting our justification has to do with *power*. If we do not claim our justification, then the power of Christ in us is never realized. It is my belief that this is the key to living theologically; that is to say, we can only acquire/realize spiritual living through the power of Christ. We can only extend grace through God's grace; only forgive through God's forgiveness, and only love because God first loved us. Rejection of justification leaves us to our own devices, which pale in comparison to the power of God. We end up struggling through the Christian life on our own power.

Without power we cannot serve, or at least without God's power, we cannot serve as well. Hebrews 12:28 tells us, "*Wherefore, receiving a kingdom (justification) that cannot be shaken, let us have grace, whereby we may offer service well-pleasing to God with reverence and awe*" (ASV). Justification is just that — accepting the kingdom of God. Our ability to live above this world comes from the realization that we no longer are of this world but rather are residents of the Kingdom of God. The Kingdom of God is here now (Mark 1:15). Through our justification we can partake in the understanding and power of his kingdom (Luke 8:10).

Athletes, who are free to perform, feel self-confident and are not distracted by imperfection. They are harder to beat. As stated earlier, the basis of sports theology is that we are originally gifted and the potential of our performance is realized in and through our relationship with God. Justification, God's willingness to continually forgive us and welcome us back, makes his power continually accessible.

Non-theological athletes are limited by their training and/or ability. They compete one dimensionally, that is to say, at one time, one place and for one reason. Christian athletes compete two-dimensionally. They compete spiritually on the field of play to glorify God and compete in the world to share their gifts as a testimony to others.

Theologically-based athletes find themselves playing or performing in a game, match, or event that is bigger than life. Being part of God's team and playing on his field is a power thing. Steve Israel, cornerback in the NFL for nine years, talks about what it means to play on God's team,

> *"Everything I do, I do for the Lord—whether it's on the field with the Patriots or off of the football field. Never be afraid to join God's team. One of my favorite verses is Philippians 4:13 which says, " 'I can do everything through Him who strengthens me.'"*

This is the basis of playing with power.

Christian athletes are able to become free of the world's pitfalls of the flesh by living their lives in the Kingdom of God. Being "justified" in Christ enables them to see God and live with a sense of peace that this world does not provide (Matthew 6:30). Being justified means that the Kingdom of God is in them (Luke 17:20). Through justification athletes are able to perform from grace, not necessity. They are able to perform based on forgiveness, not the past. They are able to perform with a sense of value, not low self-esteem. With God's forgiveness, acceptance, and the power that comes with it, they will be able to perform well and serve him successfully.

CHAPTER 4

Sanctification - Maturity

Experienced athletes understand what success is and know that failure is just part of the learning process. No matter what happens, the mature athlete views individual performance as an opportunity to play and learn at the same time.

Sanctification refers to the process by which God's grace separates man and sin, allowing man to become dedicated to God's righteousness. Sanctification results in holiness or purification from guilt and the power of sin. Justification has to do with becoming a Christian; sanctification has to do with living the Christian life. Justification is the receiving of God's power, and sanctification is putting this power to use. In justification by faith we passively receive God's grace and forgiveness. In sanctification, by God's grace, we become active servants.

Sanctification is about **growth**; it is a *process* rather than an *event* in our lives. It is how we spend our earthly days growing and learning to be Christians. To be a Christian is not about arriving at some place or reaching some perfect state of existence. Sanctification is about *spiritual growth*. It is *becoming* someone rather than *being* someone. We are always on the way (Philippians 3:12-16).

The question is: "Are you still growing?" Have you become comfortable with the growth you have behind you, or are you willing to keep changing and learning? Are you more apt to protect what you believe than push the limits of your faith? This growth, or Christian maturity if you will, is described in Ephesians 4:13-24. This passage tells us that through our faith in Christ and the "knowledge of the Son of man" we can grow in our understanding and steadfastness, which is described as the "stature of the fullness of Christ."

We have talked about the need for athletes to keep things in perspective, not to live or die on one performance or be distracted by adversity. This is easier said than done. One thing that helps is for athletes to realize that the development of their skills is a process. Tiger Woods talks about how good he can be and looks forward to getting better. I remember when he said that and the media chuckled about it because they thought he was already the best. That is probably why Tiger is Tiger and we are not.

Some have said that there is no substitute for experience. I remember back (way back) when I was playing high school football. One of our wide receivers scored a touchdown and spiked the ball and did his dance (this was before end zone celebration was an art form). When he got to the sideline, my coach took him aside and said, " Billy, when you get to the end zone in the future, act like you have been there before."

Experienced athletes understand what success is and know that failure is just part of the learning process. No matter what happens, the mature athlete views individual performance as an opportunity to play and learn at the same time. My golf coach once told me, " a bad shot tells you what you did wrong and what you need to work on. If you get so wrapped up in being angry you will miss the opportunity to learn from it and get better." This is the essence of maturity in athletics. The successful athlete grows in the good times and bad. Adversity makes the mature athlete stronger and prepares him or her for the next performance.

Because theological athletes' performance is based on faith, they understand this process. They are familiar with what maturity in Christ means, *"Therefore let us move beyond the elementary teachings about*

Christ and be taken forward to maturity, not laying again the foundation of repentance from the acts that lead to death, and faith in God" (Hebrews 6:1) (NIV). Mature Christian athletes see past the moment and understand that life is not a sprint but rather a marathon. They see each event as a step in a spiritual journey; they see each performance as a step in an athletic career.

The New Testament provides many examples of individuals who have triumphed in the face of adversity. Peter overcame his denial of Christ, Paul overcame his violent past and Jesus overcame the cross. The Christian athlete knows that he or she has not arrived; they are not perfected yet in the eyes of God. They understand this based on what Paul says, *"Brothers and sisters, I do not consider myself yet to have taken hold of it. But one thing I do: Forgetting what is behind and straining toward what is ahead*" (Philippians 3:13-14) (NIV).

Sanctification requires **action** and brings rewards. God has done His part and forgiven us; we now must respond. Once again let us return to the parable of the talents (Matthew 25:15-30). In the parable, a land-lord who was leaving the country gave his three servants five talents, two talents, and one talent according to their individual abilities. Upon the landlord's return he found that the first two servants had doubled their sums while the third had done nothing with what he had been given. The master told the third servant, *"For to everyone who has shall more be given, and he shall have abundance: but from the one who does not have, even that will be taken away."* Like the servants, those Christians who invest their God given talents and use them for his ser-vice will be rewarded. However, those who do not bear fruit for God's kingdom cannot expect to be as fulfilled as those who are faithful and follow Christ.

I am a terrible putter. I am not a bad golfer (4 handicap) in general. I just cannot putt. I am so bad that the guys I play with are always trying to console me and give me advice. The advice I usually receive is "you just need to be positive and believe that you will make the putt." I took a putting lesson once and mentioned to the pro that I had been told to just be more positive. After watching me putt for a few minutes he told me, "you can think positive all you want but if you cannot square your putter head better than that, you will never make a putt."

The problem with trying to improve athletic performance through imagery and positive thinking is that it will never overcome bad skills or technique. Telling yourself you are good does not make you good. This is the foundation of false confidence. When it comes to excellence in athletics there are no shortcuts. Thinking positively when I putt does not hurt, but faith requires action, I had better spend some time on the putting green working on my stroke.

The same is true when it comes to our faith. Saying all the right things and pretending to be religious is not the same thing as living theologically. Just as the athlete must develop the physical skills needed to perform, Christian athletes need to develop and grow in their faith. Theologically this is called sanctification.

Sanctification gives us **courage** to act, the confidence to move forward through the difficulties, dangers and obstacles of this world giving us the fortitude to be different. The courage to respond to his call (our charge) comes from God's grace and the fact that he constantly moves toward us. We alone cannot make this world a better place to live, but God can, working in and through us (John 14:12-15). The sobering thing about this charge is that, not only does God call us to action; he depends on our action to complete his work.

Winston Churchill once said, "Courage is going from failure to failure without losing enthusiasm." Edward Weeks, in reference to courage said, "To live with fear and not be afraid is the final test of maturity." I have always said that it does not take courage to sky-dive the first time but every time thereafter. Courage is not the same thing as confidence. Courage is not based on our own achievements or ability but rather is best presented when the outcome is bleak. Perseverance in the face of calamity is the breeding ground of courage. If I had to pick an athlete with confidence or an athlete with courage, I would pick the courageous athlete every time.

Above all else, courageous individuals have conviction. They believe in what they are doing; something is more important than they are. They are willing to put themselves at risk for a cause. Quite frankly, this is the big difference between theological athletes and all the rest. They prepare and compete because they were called to do so. They are called to compete just as John the Baptist was called to preach, Moses was called to lead and Jesus was called to the cross. It requires courage to "take up your cross and follow me" or to say, "Here am I Lord—send me." Christian athletes need not look far for their role model of courage. Of the original eleven disciples who carried on after Christ, ten were martyred for what they believed. This is courage born out of conviction.

Powerful performance comes with obedience to God and the reassurance that no matter the outcome, he will bless our effort. In Joshua 1:9 we read, *"Have I not commanded you? Be strong and courageous. Do not be afraid; do not be discouraged. For the Lord your God will be with you wherever you go."* (NIV) Perhaps this is the best definition of courage.

We are called to action as **humble servants** of Christ. In John 12:26 we find a good definition of a servant. The Greek word for servant is *diakonos,* which means *"to run on errands; an attendant, i.e. a waiter (at a table or in other menial duties); or specially, a Christian teacher and pastor (technically, a deacon or deaconess).* To serve means to do, no matter how grand or menial, always serving Christ. Growth and action take place together, like a child taking one step (growth) then another step (action). In any case, we should be busy for Christ.

Contemporary professional sports has brought rise to the tactic of chest beating, posturing and trash talking as an attempt to intimidate opponents. Most athletes see this behavior for what it is, an as attempt to intimidate to gain an edge. Those athletes who perform theologically do not have to resort to these tactics for an advantage. Ironically, the edge for the theological athlete comes from humility not intimidation. Confident athletes let their performance do the talking.

Sanctification (Christian maturity) allows athletes to compete from a position of strength, knowing that they are prepared and ordained to perform by God.

These athletes are *complete* and free to *compete*. Christian athletes are not concerned about themselves, which allows them to focus on the task that lies ahead. It has been said, "Being humble is not thinking less of yourself, it is thinking of yourself less." Tom Lehman was quoted to say, " Just because you're competitive, that doesn't mean you're not a Christian. Christians can compete with anyone at any time. Meek doesn't mean weak."

Humility allows us to serve. The Christian athlete knows that any particular gift is given to serve God and others, not for their own glory. They perform for, and are committed to, a greater purpose. Humility and strength go hand in hand. Jesus Christ is the theological athlete's model when it comes to being strong and humble. Jesus modeled this when he washed the feet of the disciples, and no one would accuse Jesus of being weak. Mark 10:45 explains Jesus' motivation. *"For even the Son of Man did not come to be served. But to serve, and to give his life as a ransom for many"*(NIV).

Humility does not change the *way* the game is played; the power for this athlete comes from *why* the game is played — to serve God. Torri Hunter, seven-time Golden Glove Winner for the Los Angeles Angels, talks about why he performs when he says, "I think about that a lot, being out there, you've got a chance to shine. You've got a chance to let people know your Christian testimony and everything about it and let them know that you follow God. What is greater than that?" John Smoltz of the Atlanta Braves once said, "I would love to leave a legacy with my children to know that God had a hand in my life, to know that he changed me from a decent person to a God-fearing, loving person, with a servant mind-set, humility, who thinks of others before himself."

Performance is enhanced when an athlete is able to see past the moment, and view competition as part of something greater than "self." I think Jim Tressel, Head Football Coach of Ohio State University, best describes the connection between athletics and service when he says, "My vision is to constantly seek to know what God's will is for my life and follow that, and not write my own script. I am here to serve others, and not simply myself."

The power, or miracle if you will, is that we are transformed as servants. We now serve to *please,* not *appease,* God. This is the practical difference between grace and works theology. The Christian life is not a burden that we must accept as toil. As Christians, God's will is not something we must obey to avoid his wrath. God's will is now our will — not rules that condemn us. His will becomes a foundation of faith that sets us free (Romans 3: 21-27).

Through God's power and sanctification we are **changed.** There are many ways to describe this change. The verb "to sanctify" means "to make holy." A Christian is by definition "being made holy." Most Christians cringe when they hear that they are to live holy lives, with their minds jumping from "saint" to "super human," from "holy" to "holier-than-thou," from "sanctified" to "sanctimonious."

When holiness comes to mind we think of people who live their lives by a list of thou "shall nots" and attempt to obey these rules to feel superior. The key here is to realize that we cannot be holy without the sense of sin and God's grace and forgiveness. We are not perfect as God is perfect (Philippians 3:12). Holiness for us means "set apart", not perfect or even deserving, but yet consecrated. We are the new tribe of Levi (Deuteronomy 10:8).

We are called to live holy lives in this world. We are not removed from the world around us but rather are beacons of light in a dark world (Matthew 5:15-16). Christians are called to demonstrate the power and love that prevents us from succumbing to the standards of this world. It is not enough to say what we believe but rather it is by faith and action that Christians are set apart (stand out).

Theologically, it is in the realm of sanctification that true worship occurs. Sanctification allows us to use our gifts and claim what we have been promised —both are to be used to glorify Him. What we believe, what we understand and how we see our role in this life, takes place in relationship to sanctification. When we are sanctified, we respond to God's call and then demonstrate our desire to please our Lord.

Through God's power and sanctification we are transformed. Someone once said to me that the power of God is not seen in the moving of mountains but in the changing of hearts. We have talked about some of the advantages of performing from a spiritual or theological perspective such as confidence, courage, power, maturity etc. The difference between talking the talk and walking the walk is a changed heart. Christian athletes do not just appear to be different, they are different—they have been transformed.

The Christian athlete not only desires to follow Christ, through sanctification, he or she now has the power to do so. This transformation is described and promised in 2 Corinthians 3:16-18, which reads,

> *"But whenever I turn to the Lord, the veil is taken away. Now the Lord is the Spirit: and where the Spirit of the Lord is, (there) is liberty. But we all, with unveiled face beholding as in a mirror the glory of the Lord, are transformed into the same image from glory to glory, even as from the Lord the Spirit." (ASV)*

Therefore, the Christian athlete is changed, not into someone new, but returned to his or her original condition—in the image of God. Once again, this is the basis of sports theology. This transformation allows athletes to demonstrate God's gifts without the distractions of the flesh. The Christian athlete can now identify with the blind man healed by Christ, "*...I was blind but now I see*" (John 9:25) (ASV).

Every athlete wants to be the best. No kid in the back yard or at practice fantasizes about making the final shot to come in second. It is human nature to want to feel good about who we are, be the center of attention or receive the accolades of others. We all want our five minutes of fame (most want more). How many times have you heard an athlete at the top of their profession say that their career will not be complete until they win a national title, the Super Bowl or the Pennant? It is a fact that all athletes (at any level) want to be number one.

Athletes who compete spiritually know God has sanctified them, they are "set apart." Athletes who perform for God have already won the Super Bowl, they have not only received five minutes of fame, they have received eternal life. They are not only complete as athletes; they are complete as individuals.

It would be a mistake to think that Christian athletes perform with less determination because they are pursuing spiritual fulfillment. Every time a team plays for a championship for the first time against a defending champion, the media asks if this will make a difference. The coach of the defending champion team always says, "Yes, it helps if you have been here before." Christian athletes who play theologically have been there and have been victorious. They have played on a bigger stage with much more at stake. They will be ready to perform.

Being sanctified allows Christian athletes to be free from their sinful nature and reach their spiritual potential. They are able to see that all things, good or bad, can be used to help them grow in their faith. They become aware of God's call to arms and are filled with confidence and courage — courage, which does not come from them, but through the transformation of living their lives based on God's will. Christian athletes perform to serve and understand that their athletic gift is a chance to share God's Word with others.

CHAPTER 5

Peace – Pressure

"Choke" is like the word "shank" in golf — there seems to be a superstition that if you do not say it, it won't happen.

Being a Christian should improve our lives, provide us with strength and bring a sense of joy and peace. Most Christians are familiar with Psalms 23. Unfortunately we can get caught up in the "*yea, though I walk through the valley of the shadow of death*" and think that the passage is about the fear of dying. Sure, that is part of it, but the meat of this passage describes the good life of the sheep — it is about living in **peace**. The sheep have all they need: food, water and protection. They are assured of a peaceful life; they have nothing to fear. Trouble starts when sheep (we) wander off. God continually desires and attempts to take care of us; we put ourselves at risk when we move away from him. In John 10: 7-11 we find one of the most important promises of Christ when he says,

> "*Verily, verily, I say unto you, I am the door of the sheep. All that came before me enter in, he shall be saved, and shall go in and go out, and shall find pasture. The thief cometh not, but that he may steal, and kill, and destroy: I came that they may have life, and may have it abundantly. I am the good shepherd: the good shepherd layeth down his life for the sheep*" (ASV).

It is clear to me that in this passage we see that the "abundant life" is a life free from fear and anxiety. From this text we can also see that peace in life comes, not from what we can do, but from the protection of

Christ. Problems come when being a sheep is not enough for us and we start wanting to be the shepherd (Adam's issue).

I often ask my clients if they could have one thing what would it be. Almost to the person, the answer is the same, happiness. When asked to elaborate, they tend to ramble and struggle to articulate what "happy" means. When I say, "Do you mean peace?" they reply, "Yes, that is what I mean." The frequency of this reply tells me that as individuals we intrinsically know the difference between the temporal and the spiritual. For me, this is one of those statements that prove we are spiritual beings.

Hang around athletes for any length of time and you will hear plenty of "four- letter " words. One five-letter word you will not hear much is the word "choke." Johnny Miller used the word choke as a golf announcer and you would have thought he had cursed his mother on national television. Choke is like the word "shank" in golf — there seems to be a superstition that if you do not say it, it won't happen. In Miller's defense he just said what most athletes fear the most — that they will fold under the pressure.

A large part of sports psychology attempts to teach techniques that allow athletes to perform under pressure. Concepts like imagery, positive thinking, anchoring and arousal are taught to increase performance under pressure. In contrast, sports theology allows the athlete to perform under pressure, by being at peace.

The reason why most people pick peace over happiness is because they know that peace brings

contentment. A client once told me that he was plagued with the "curse of discontentment." As he explained this inability to be satisfied the more I realized how powerful and prevalent discontentment is. Happiness is a human term that describes a feeling, not a state of being. The New Testament never promises a continual state of happiness in this world but it does promise that we can be content through Christ. This is what Paul says in Philippians 4:11, *"I am not saying this because I am in need, for I have learned to be content in whatever the circumstances"* (NIV). Once again Paul talks about contentment in Hebrews13: 5-6, when he says,

> *"Keep your lives free from the love of money and be content with what you have, because God has said, 'never will I leave you, never will I forsake you.' So we say with confidence, the Lord is my helper, I will not be afraid. What can human beings do to me?" (NIV)*

Christian contentment does not mean that we have to settle for whatever comes. It does not mean that we should allow others to take advantage of us just because we are Christians. In fact the opposite is true. As seen in the passage above, being content breeds confidence, and confidence helps us set boundaries. Contentment means that we are complete no matter how we are treated. There is a big difference.

When it comes to dealing with pressure, sports psychology and sports theology have the same goals, to minimize the pressure and increase the athlete's ability to be calm in the midst of this pressure. In sports theology both of these goals are approached by the personal contentment that comes from God's promise of peace. Athletes at the highest level have already demonstrated that they can handle the pressure that comes with performing. They have been in big games in their lives. They have excelled when the pressure was on or they would not have reached the top of their profession.

In my view, the key in performing under pressure is not in trying to minimize it, just don't exacerbate it. Mechanically, the three-foot put is not any harder to make to win a tournament than it is in practice. The pressure increases, not because the putt is harder; it becomes harder because of what the putt means.

The Christian athlete plays with a sense of peace and contentment that does not rely of the outcome of a putt or any other play or shot. They are complete and fulfilled through God's love no matter the outcome. 1 Thessalonians 5:23 says, "... *Now may the God of peace himself sanctify you completely; and may your whole spirit, soul, and body be preserved* "(NKJV). Athletes who perform spiritually have all they need, or better yet, have nothing to lose. Trey Johnston, of the San Diego Padres was quoted to say,

> *"I have let go of all my control of my life and gave it to Christ. He is now in total control of my life and he is working his awesome power. My body no longer aches, I never feel alone, and I am filled with an indescribable joy."*

The spiritual athlete does not have to learn techniques in the attempt to be confident in the face of pressure. Athletes like Trey are content, and can compete with a sense of peace. This is victory in and over pressure.

Being at peace means feeling **safe.** No matter what befalls us as Christians we are safe. Just as a sheep cannot protect itself, we cannot feel safe without God. It is through our relationship with him, and faith in his love for us, that safety is found, *"The Lord will rescue me from every evil attack and will bring me safely to his heavenly kingdom. To him be the glory for ever and ever"*(2 Timothy 4:18) (NIV). Feeling safe or protected does not come from being in control, being smart or from being free of the dangers of the world. It comes from knowing that what ever the world brings, nothing is more powerful than God's love for us.

Like the sheep, we put ourselves at risk when we strike out on our own and leave the protection of the shepherd (God). Somewhere in our fallen nature we believe we are better off on our own. This is faulty thinking for two reasons. First, and foremost, we do not know as much as we think. 1 Corinthians 13:12 says, " *For now we see in a mirror, dimly, but then face to face. Now I know in part, but then I shall know just as I also am known* (ASV). We convince ourselves that we know what is best, where we are going and how we will get there. Unfortunately we are seeing life through a "knot hole" which limits our view. We end up making bad decisions based on a limited view.

Secondly, this false confidence prevents us from knowing that we are lost in the first place. It limits our ability to rely of God's knowledge and understanding which provides the protection that we originally desired. As stated above in 2 Timothy 4:18, God has to "rescue" us, sometimes even against our will.

Arousal is a term that is often used in sports psychology that refers to ones level of anxiety about a past, present, or future event. There are two types of arousal: (1) *Trait arousal* is your own personal "normal" level - it's just how excited you usually are; (2) *State arousal* is the level at which you function during important and stressful events. As with most functions, there is an appropriate and helpful level of arousal and a dysfunctional level. Being overly anxious is seldom useful in performance.

Anyone who has attempted to stretch a single into a double in baseball knows the feeling of reaching second base safely. As time is called and the ball goes back to the pitcher, there is a feeling of peace and calmness that was not there when the runner rounded first. All of the anxiety and pressure (for the moment) is gone. The goal of any athlete is to feel this sense of peace and calmness when the pressure is on; to know that whatever happens he will be safe. Athletes who live their lives relying on God's love and protection realize that this feeling of peace and safety can be continual. They do not have to learn a technique to remain calm in the midst of pressure; they have experienced peace in their daily lives. They know that, *"The name of the Lord is a fortified tower, the righteous run to it and are safe"*(Proverbs 18:10) (NIV).

The athlete who plays under God's protection is free to put his or her energies into performance rather than in self-preservation. They can perform with the joy that Trey Johnston talked about. They can participate, in the moment and for the moment, under the protection of God' s watchful eye. They are safe for eternity. John Kasay of the Carolina Panthers, talks about playing from an eternal point of view when he says,

> " I know I am a child of God and will go to heaven and spend eternity with him. I am able to live each day with peace in my heart, living a life that seeks to please God for his gift of eternal life - not because I'm trying to earn his approval, but because I love him and desire to do his will."

The Christian athlete is guarded by God and lives not out of fear but on the hope that comes with his protection,

> "Then your face will brighten in innocence. You will be strong and free of fear. You will forget your misery. It will all be gone like water under the bridge. Your life will be brighter than the noonday. Any darkness will be as bright as morning. You will have courage because you will have hope. You will be protected and will rest in safety" (Job 11:15-18) (NLT).

Living at peace helps us when it comes to managing **stress**. My definition of stress is: a*ny internal or* *external situation or process that negatively affects one's emotional health or quality of life.* It is impossible to live without stress. Stress is not inherently bad. What some people call stress others might call a challenge. This is why in my definition I use the words "negatively affects" to distinguish appropriate stress from bad stress. Stress that negatively affects us is seen as a threat, something that puts us at risk.

There is a big difference in living at risk (stressed) and living in peace. Risk-based living puts us on our heels and makes us defensive while feeling safe allows us to lean into life, looking for opportunities. If we constantly feel unprotected and exposed then life becomes stressful. If I am allergic to bee stings then I am afraid of everything that buzzes. No matter how appropriate or inappropriate this fear is, one thing for sure, it changes my view of picnics.

Stress comes at us from two directions; it comes at us externally and internally. External stress comes from our environment. These stressors are things like deadlines, traffic, financial obligations and other pressures brought on by the world. Internal stress refers to the pressures we put on ourselves like personal expectations, worry, various unresolved feelings and insecurities. Traditional stress management attempts to teach individuals to identify particular stressors and then use "self talk" techniques to approach each stressor with confidence. This is easier said than done.

In my experience, the best stress management approach comes from living on the promises of Christ. It is difficult for individuals, who see life as dangerous or who are perfectionistic, to just change. We need help. This help is found in l John 14:26-27,

> *"But the Comforter, (even) the Holy Spirit, whom the Father will send in my name, he shall teach you all things, and bring to your remembrance all that I said unto you. Peace I leave with you; my peace I give unto you: not as the world giveth, give I unto you. Let not your heart be troubled, neither let it be fearful"* (ASV).

God does not want us to live under stress. He does not want us to be distracted by worry and fear. We are told this in Matthew 6:34, *"Be not therefore anxious for tomorrow: for tomorrow will be anxious for itself. Each day has enough trouble of its own"* (NIV). God wants us healthy, focused and available to use the gifts he has given us.

As we have mentioned, stress is all around us. In our previous discussion we have specifically related theology to athletic performance. Although it has been understood from the beginning, we need to acknowledge that athletes are real people too. They have lives outside of athletics; they too must manage the stress that comes with life in general. Athletes, like the rest of us, have to deal with stress on two levels; they must manage everyday stress and the stress that comes with athletic performance. For athletes, the inability to deal with stress on either one of these fronts may hinder performance; the inability to handle stress on both levels simultaneously, certainly does. Simply put, athletes at the highest level need to be experts at stress management. The good news is that all stress can be managed through the same thing, through the peace that comes from God.

Living ours lives based on the principles and promises that Christ has given us is all we need to live stress free. We have said that living spiritually allows us to give up control, live without fear and calm our worries. These skills are the foundation of any stress management program. When it comes to stress, peace is not only the solution it is also the outcome. The Christian athlete who relies on the " Prince of Peace" will be at peace.

Victory over stress comes from changing our lives through Christ and not from simply changing our environment. Bryan Bullington of the Pittsburgh Pirates talks about the personal transformation that allows him to deal with stress when he says,

> " For the first time in my life, I really started reading the Bible, and exploring what God was all about. In the past two years, I have grown a lot as a person and as a Christian. Coming to the realization that I cannot be in control of everything that happens in my life has been very comforting to me. It felt like a huge weight was lifted off of my shoulders. It is amazing how much happier I am now."

Theologically-based athletes handle external stress by knowing that God will protect them and deal with internal stress by knowing that God unconditionally loves them. This is the ground floor of living in peace.

Living our lives filled with joy and peace (Romans 15:13) allows us the opportunity to **rest**. When I am working with a client who is overwhelmed in life and desires peace, we turn to Psalms 46:10, which says, *"Be still, and know that I am God: I will be exalted among the nations, I will be exalted in the earth"* (ASV). In this passage the Greek word for *be still* means "to slacken" or "cease." In plain language, this verse tells us *to cut ourselves some slack and let God be God.* It tells us to take a break, relax and rest — God has got it!

We are told in Matthew 11:28, *"Come unto me, all ye that labor and are heavy laden, and I will give you rest"* (ASV). As usual, the problem is not that God is unwilling to help; the problem is that we just don't accept it. For us to give our worries and stress to God requires just two things. We first have to believe he will take them and secondly, we have to actually let them go. In my experience God usually does not grab our worries from us, we have to give them to him. We have to overcome our need for control and live on faith.

It is the difference between living life in the flesh and living our lives theologically. It is the difference in living on our own power and living a restful life. It is the difference in carrying our own yoke and putting on the yoke of God, *"Take my yoke upon you, and learn from me; for I am meek and lowly in heart: and ye shall find rest unto your souls. For my yoke is easy, and my burden is light"* (Matthew 11:29-30) (ASV).

Living in peace allows us to rest. It may sound silly but many athletes need to be given permission to rest.   Someone once told me that Benjamin Franklin hated to sleep due to fact that he was already "limited by the 24-hour day" and there was too much left to invent. Edgar Allen Poe once said, 'Sleep, those little slices of death, how I loath them." During my clinical training as a hospital chaplain I ran across an individual like this. The day after quadruple by-pass surgery he was complaining that the phone had been taken out of his room and he had business to conduct. Believe me when I say that some people can't stop!

How many times have we been watching a basketball game and the commentator says, "This game is getting out of control, their coach needs to call a time-out." Every athlete knows how quickly pressure subsides when a player or coach calls time-out. In essence that is what rest is, time to regroup, recover and re-evaluate. God even rested. In Exodus 31:17 we are told, *"Jehovah made heaven and earth, and on the seventh day he rested, and was refreshed."*

Athletes need rest, and this just doesn't mean, "taking five" after wind sprints. The Hebrew word for *refreshed* in Exodus 31:17 literally means, "to take a breath" or "to breathe fresh air." In modern terms we would tell someone who is upset to, "take a deep breath and calm down." We have all heard someone in the midst of an argument say, "I need to get some fresh air." In these examples the individual does not need to rest physically, but rather needs an emotional break. In both cases the individual seeks peace.

Those who make a living in sports know the importance of being "fresh" when it comes to excellence in performance. Tiger Woods does not play in every event he can. College teams value the off week and strategically schedule them before the biggest game. Teams use substitution to insure that there are "fresh legs" on the field or court. Coaches and athletes know that fatigue can be as formidable as any opponent.

Athletes who perform theologically have permission and the ability to rest continually. They do not have to ask an official or referee for time-out. These athletes play on a higher plane for a higher purpose, which provides them with a sense of calm and peace even in the midst of competition. God is their official and "time" can be called at any time. Playing for God not only gives us permission to rest, he promises it, "*Whoever dwells in the shelter of the Most High will rest in the shadow of the Almighty*" (Psalms 91:1)(NIV).

Living our lives founded on God's promise of peace allows us to handle **pressure** in general. Webster defines peace as: *a state of tranquility or quiet: freedom for disquieting or oppressive thoughts or emotions.* Just as stress is not always bad, pressure is often times appropriate. With any job that requires responsibility there is pressure in varying degrees.

God's peace allows us to not only handle the major stressors in our lives it also helps us with the less dramatic, less threatening pressures of daily living. Being at peace does not take pressure away, it allows us to be tranquil in its midst. Peace allows us to negotiate the trials, tribulations and pressures of life by feeling safe and rested. Most importantly, peace allows us to be *still*.

One could argue that peace is the opposite of pressure and true peace, comes from God. No matter what the pressure is or where it comes from, it can be overcome through reliance on him. When it comes to pressure, as in all things, God's gift of peace gives Christian athletes an advantage. They live above the pressure of this world. They are content, free from stress, safe and refreshed, none of which is threatened by their performance or the outcome of a contest.

The constant feeling of well being that comes from God's protection and love allows athletes to play the game for the game's sake. Peace does not come from performance; performance is enhanced because there is a sense of peace. Jamey Carroll of the Cleveland Indians, talks about playing above the pressure when he says,

> *"I think it made me understand that God is in control. In this game a lot of things are thrown at you. There's a lot of pressure to succeed, and when you try to control that on your own, you just make it tougher on yourself. And as you grow, you play to glorify Him. You use the abilities that He's given you to play for Him."*

The only pressure on Christian athletes is to make sure they avoid distractions from God's call, not that they will miss the ball.

Living our lives under the watchful eye of a loving God fills us with joy and peace. We, like the sheep in Psalms 23, are content. This contentment comes from feeling safe and protected and enables us to negotiate the stress and pressure of everyday life. This constant sense of well-being allows us to rest and recover emotionally and physically. Feeling safe and secure allows athletes to focus on God's purpose and increases their ability to perform.

CHAPTER 6

Providence (God's Plan) – Game Plan

I am not saying that it is always easy to feel Gods love, but some individuals live each day unaware of the possibility. For these people, God seems far away, and their faith does not provide them with a sense of his closeness and support.

Theologically, **providence** refers to God's continuous activity in his creation. The term providence refers to how active God is in the world and in our lives. Denial of this concepts means that the universe is governed by chance and chaos. Providence is the theological doctrine that answers questions like: "Does God really pay attention to me and is he with me on a daily basis?" "Is he really *in it* with me?" "Does he care about my pain and sorrow?" "Does he rejoice in my triumphs?"

Through providence comes the assurance that we are never out of God's sight, *"They all know that the Lord has done this. For the life of every living thing is in his hand, and the breath of all humanity"* (Job 12:9-10) (NLT). In John 11:33-35 we see how much Jesus cared about Lazarus when he died,

> *"When Jesus therefore saw her weeping, and the Jews (also) weeping who came with her, he groaned in the spirit, and was troubled, and said, Where have ye laid him? They say unto him, Lord, come and see. Jesus wept" (ASV).*

In Isaiah 62:5 we are told that God celebrates with us in the living of our lives, *"…then God will rejoice over you as a bridegroom rejoices over his bride"*(NLT).

I am not saying that it is always easy to feel Gods love, but some individuals live each day unaware of the possibility. For these people, God seems far away, and their faith does not provide them with a sense of his closeness and support. Acts 17:27 tells us: *"That they should seek God, if they seek Him they might feel after him and find him, He is not far from each one of us"* (ASV). The power of God's providence comes down to our ability/choice to take advantage of the promises of God.

Providence means that *God has a plan, we are active in it and he is active in our part of it.* We are told about God's plan in Ephesians 1:11, *"In Him we were also chosen, having been predestined according to the plan of Him who works everything in conformity with the purpose of His will"* (NIV). We see that we are part of God's plan in Proverbs 16:19 *"In their hearts human beings plan their course, but the Lord establishes their steps"* (NIV). We are not alone in our part of his plan, *"You gave me life and showed me kindness, and in your providence watched over my spirit"*(Job10: 12) (NIV). As we have said, "we were made on purpose for a purpose."

It is through the concept of providence that we talk about God's will (plan). The Greek word for "will" is *thelema,* which means *determination, choice, inclination or purpose.* When we talk about God's plan, we are talking about his determined will. I do not understand why so many people are confused and feel that God's will is hidden, complicated or encrypted. Jesus is very clear as to what God's will is in John 6:40. He tells us *"For this is the will of my Father, that every one that beholdeth the Son, and believeth on him should have eternal life; and I will raise him up on the last day"* (ASV). It is plain that God's will is to bring us back to him for eternity. Our salvation *is* God's will. This is why

Jesus tells us not to fear those that can kill the body but to fear the one who can kill both body and soul (Matthew 10:28).

Unfortunately, for many Christians, God's will tends to be vague and/or elusive. When I ask my clients to describe God's will, they usually struggle. The truth is that many of us talk about wanting to know God's will for our lives, yet we do not even know what "God's will" means. God's will means his plan for our lives and the guarantee that he has equipped us to do it.

Christian athletes who embrace God's will as their own can stop worrying about the small things. By putting God first they are free, through faith, to relax and perform knowing that he is in control. Seth Franco of the Harlem Globetrotters is talking about trusting God's will when he says, *"Whenever God places you somewhere you can find the grace and strength to be effective right there. The Globetrotters were not an end, but a stepping stone to what God has in mind for me."*

Only when we understand God's will can we become part of it. This is the point where we tend to get lost. Many Christians seem to struggle with knowing or articulating their individual place in God's will. I often hear Christians asking themselves, "What is God's will for my life?" or "What can I do to be in God's will?" How many times have you heard people repeatedly say that they are praying for God to show them his will for their lives?

We have to be careful that we do not determine what we want and then attempt to convince ourselves that this is God's will. When we do this, and we all do, we limit God and our potential. Athletes who attempt to define God's will by how they play or if they win or lose, are thinking too small. God's will is bigger and more meaningful than that.

Many times Christians question God's will because they are unhappy or are overwhelmed by the struggles of life. Somewhere along the way these individuals started to believe that being in God's will means an easier life, a life free of pain, tragedy, loss and hardship. Some Christians believe that if they get outside God's will then bad things happen and, conversely, if they are in God's will good things happen. This causes what I call "God's will hunting." The game then becomes trying to spot God's will and get in it for self-protection or personal benefit. This of course is not what God's will is all about.

We do not seek God's will for our benefit, nor should we evaluate our place in his will by our earthly circumstances. We tend to get confused because we have somehow interpreted God's will to be some type of key to decision making, i.e., one choice being in God's will and the other not. We tell ourselves, "If I could only determine God's will, then I would know what to do." God's will is not about knowing everything; it is about salvation.

God never promised us that following him would make things easier in this world. This fact is supported in Job's life, in Paul's multiple imprisonments and in the wanderings of the Israelites in the wilderness. The deaths of the martyred disciples or most visibly, Jesus' crucifixion, demonstrate that life is not always easy. The fact of the matter is that following Christ can mark us for persecution (2 Timothy 3:12). In Romans 8:35 Paul tells us "*Who shall separate us from the love of Christ? Shall tribulation, or anguish, or persecution, or famine, or nakedness, or peril, or sword?*" I think that Paul would be the first to say that life on earth was difficult and yet we do not question his ability to follow God's will.

Athletes benefit from this understanding of God's will. There is often no connection between our faith or value and the bad things that happen. Knowing Christ does not mean that the ball will always bounce their way or they will always prevail in competition. If this were so then God would have to play favorites. Living out of the Christian faith does not control the outcome of an event, but our relationship with Christ determines how we handle the outcome.

It is my belief that our confusion about the will of God comes from our selfish nature. Once again we have taken God's plan and tried to make it revolve around our needs. In essence we have once again taken something simple and made it difficult. Now I know that most Christians want to do what God desires and want to please him. Jesus struggled with this battle between his flesh and God's will in the Garden of Gethsemane (Luke 22:42). Here in the midst of the ultimate worldly test, Jesus says, "not my will but thine be done." While the Jews were plotting to kill Jesus, he told his disciples, "*I can of myself do nothing: as I hear, I judge: and my judgment is righteous; because I seek not mine own will, but the will of him that sent me. If I bear witness of myself, my witness is not true*"(John 5:30-31) (ASV).

Jesus was not confused about his will versus the will of God: the two were/are the same. God's will, which was to make himself known to those who were lost, became the will of Jesus. This path should also be the will of those who follow him. The difference between the human Jesus and us is that he always followed God's will, not his own.

Over the years I have started to believe that the word "will" in God's will not only refers to God's purpose but can also mean *inheritance*. In this sense "will" means: *A legal declaration of a person's wishes regarding the disposal of his or her property or estate.* In Matthew 25:34 we are told, *"Come ye blessed of the Father, inherit the kingdom prepared for you from the foundation of the world"* (ASV). Matthew 19: 29 tells us that everyone that follows Christ will inherit eternal life or, as Paul says in Hebrews 6:12, *"...but imitators of them who through faith and patience inherit the promises"* (ASV).

Defining God's will in this way allows us to stop trying to find something that we already have. In this interpretation God's will is not allusive or something that can be lost by making mistakes or bad decisions. God does not write us in and out of his will based on our behavior or performance. Through our relationship with Christ we are in his will for eternity. The New Testament is clear about this.

No matter how you define the will of God, it is powerful. God, the creator of all things, will not fail, *"For since the creation of the world God's invisible qualities – his eternal power and divine nature – have been clearly seen..."* (Romans 1:20) (NIV). Those who follow God's will, who align their lives with the desires of God, likewise cannot fail.

In the beginning of this chapter we said that providence is the theological doctrine that answers questions like: "Does God really pay attention to me and what I am doing on a daily basis?" "Is he really *in it* with me?" "Does he care about my pain and sorrow?" "Does he rejoice in my triumphs?" These are fair questions, especially for athletes in the heat of competition. Christian athletes know that the answers to all these questions are "yes." They know this because they understand that God has a plan, they are part of his plan and he helps them in their part of this plan.

God's plan is to return mankind to him for eternity. That is what he is about and what he values above all else. The Christian athlete who plays and lives for Christ has the same goal and lives his or her life accordingly. We have said many times that the Christian athlete plays on a larger field and has a bigger perspective. The difference for the theological athlete is that he or she performs out of service and from a position of strength that comes from participating in God's will.

Once again I am reminded of a line in the movie Tin Cup. When describing the golf swing Roy McAvoy says, "*The golf swing is about letting go and holding on at the same time.*" This is both a good description of living in God's will and good advice when it comes to athletic performance. Living in God's will allows athletes to focus on their job and let God focus on his. By holding on to the promises of Christ these athletes can let go of the petty worries and distractions that the world brings. Even though we may not always know what God is doing or where he is taking us, there is a sense of freedom and peace in following him.

This sense of spiritual well being in the midst of conflict is huge for the athlete. Performing spiritually allows the athlete to understand that whatever happens, it happens on a small scale. Athletes who align their goals with God's plan see any setback as temporal and relatively insignificant. Setbacks are temporal because Gods plan is eternal; these setbacks are insignificant because they cannot separate us from his love. Trusting in God's plan allow athletes to perform with confidence and less pressure. This may be the purist demonstration of faith.

One thing that makes Christianity unique is the relationship between the Creator and the created. This is not only unique but also significant. One of the most dynamic elements in being in relationship with God revolves around free choice. God's giving man free choice not only demonstrates his desire for a relationship, it communicates that he values us as individuals. As in any relationship of depth and value there needs to be mutual consent, and this does not exist unless there is free choice on the part of both parties.

Inherent in any significant relationship there is risk. The risk in relationships comes from each person having free choice. The nature of healthy relationships is such that the level of intimacy is directly related to equality and the freedom to leave or stay. In giving there is risk and no assurance that you will receive. God loves us enough to risk losing us, which says a lot about him, how he feels about us, and the importance of this relationship.

The good news is that God loves us enough to give us free choice; the bad news is that with free choice comes accountability. Christians cannot accept the freedom to choose on the one hand and then blame God for the consequences of their bad choices on the other. Some Christians would give up free choice to avoid personal accountability. They would rather have God tell them what to do so mistakes would not be made. Unfortunately for them it doesn't work that way. In reality, they would all rail against God if he told us everything to do!

Athletes who live their lives spiritually embrace free choice and the accountability that comes with it. They understand that true glorification of God can only come from voluntary acts. Doing what God says because we have to is not the same as doing God's will by choice. There is no glorification of God in having been *given* gifts; what we choose to *do* with those gifts is what glorifies him.

Another uniqueness of Christianity is that God relies on us to help fulfill his purpose. We are not simple inanimate objects that are created for his pleasure. He trusts us enough and depends on us to help him achieve his purpose, which is to save souls (the great commission), *"Go ye therefore, and make disciples of all the nations, baptizing them in the name of the Father and of the Son and of the Holy Spirit"* (Matthew 28:19-20) (ASV).

Any athlete, who is called on to take the last shot, kick the winning kick or swim anchor, knows what it is like to feel valuable. Athletically, to have your name called when the game is on the line is the ultimate compliment. This kind of recognition tells the athlete that others believe that they are prepared, skilled and willing to take on the pressure of the moment. They understand what this means about their value and how important they are to the team.

Christian athletes understand how this feels everyday. On or off the field they feel valuable because God is calling their names. They are not just being called to perform but to share the "good news" to those around by simply performing. Being called by God to help fulfill his purpose is a tremendous responsibility and demonstrates God's confidence in these athletes. Michael Redd of the Milwaukee Bucks says,

> " I think that [was] my purpose, other than just to shoot the basketball, it gives me the chance to let others know about Christ and help them through situations they may be going through. I thank God for the opportunity and the privilege to share the gospel in no matter what setting..."

In a sense the Christian athlete is playing two games; he or she is competing on two levels simultaneously. One level is on the field or court and the other is on the spiritual level of the "upward call of Jesus Christ" (Philippians 3:14). Every athlete has heard the saying that "It is not if you win or lose it is how you play the game." Many athletes think this saying is laughable. But the Christian athlete knows the truth in this quote. They know that when you play for God, how you play is where the glory is. They understand this through 1 Corinthians 9:24, which says, "*Do you not know that in a race all the runners run, but only one gets the prize? Run in such a way as to get the prize"* (NIV).

We have talked about the first two parts of providence, which are God's plan and our part in that plan. The last part of providence refers to his helping us with our part. God does not call us to help him and then leave us high and dry. God's involvement and help is seen in the promise of the coming of Christ, *"Therefore the Lord himself will give you a sign: behold, a virgin shall conceive, and bear a son, and shall call his name Immanuel"* (Isaiah 7:14)(ASV). The Hebrew word for Immanuel literally means "God with us." After His resurrection Jesus promises not to abandon us, *"But the Advocate, the Holy Spirit, whom the Father will send in my name, will teach you all things and will remind you of everything I have said to you"* (John 14:26) (NIV). We are not alone.

We have been uniquely made. We all have been given individual skills (gifts) for a specific reason — to spread God's word. We are unique, not to be *independent* but rather to function better *interdependently*. Each one of us has a particular part to play in the completion of God's will,

> *"But you are a chosen people, a royal priesthood, a holy nation, God's special possession, that you may declare the praises of him who called you out of darkness into his wonderful light"* (1 Peter 2:9) (NIV).

As a matter of fact, He has provided us with the skills to perform long before we are called to serve. We all have unique skills and experiences, and we have work to do.

Athletes who perform theologically never perform alone. As I said earlier God does not call us to service and then abandon us. Would you spend hours in the back yard throwing the baseball with your child and then never watch him/her play? Do we expect less from God? Let us not forget that God was concerned for and searched for Adam even in the midst of disobedience. Luke 12:6-7 tells us where we stand with God, " *Are not five sparrows sold for two pence? And not one of them is forgotten in the sight of God. But the very hairs of your head are all numbered. Fear not: ye are of more value than many sparrows.*"

God does not only *know us* individually he is *in us*. Christian athletes do not just perform knowing that God is watching them; they perform with the Holy Spirit in them. This fact alone should sell an athlete on sports theology. Athletes who understand and actualize the Holy Spirit have unlocked their potential to perform. They have been transformed into new men and women with unlimited possibilities and power. This is one of the most powerful, yet overlooked, promises in Christendom, *"But you shall receive power (ability, efficiency, and might) when the Holy Spirit has come upon you…."* (Acts 1:8) (AMP).

Living and performing through the Holy Spirit is the foundation of sports theology and impacts every aspect of athletic success. No matter if you are talking about lack of confidence, poor preparation, fear or succumbing to pressure they all are overcome through a relationship with the Holy Spirit. Psalms 20:6 tells us, *"Now this I know: The Lord gives victory to his anointed. He answers him from his heavenly sanctuary with the victorious power of his right hand"*(NIV). The Christian athlete is confident, prepared, unafraid and less stressed because they perform knowing, *"For the Lord your God is the one who goes with you to fight for you against your enemies to give you victory"* (Deuteronomy 20:4) (NIV).

CHAPTER 7

Revelation - Potential

Contrary to what some Christians may think, God is not vague, mysterious or shy about disclosing who he is. He not only tells us who he is, he shows us. His words and actions agree. When he acts, he explains what he is doing with an interpretive word.

The Christian doctrine of **revelation** is two-fold in nature. First, it refers to God's communication to man concerning himself, his moral standards, and his plan of salvation. Secondly, it reveals the characteristics of man to man himself. In other words, the study of God (theology) is getting to know God and learning more about ourselves.

God reveals himself. This a powerful truth which means that we do not have to learn who God is on our own or search him out, he confronts us with himself, person to person. To "know God" does not mean to know about him, to believe intellectually and grasp rationally that there is a God, or to have information about him and his will. To know God is to *experience* him. To know God is to acknowledge him, confess him, honor him and do his will.

Webster defines revelation as: *1 a: an act of revealing or communicating divine truth b: something that is revealed by God to humans.* By this definition we can see that revelation is about "revealed truth" which is not limited to just truth about God. In my years as a Christian therapist I have found that many times we may know less about ourselves than we know about God. As in any relationship, we need to understand both parties.

Although many people believe that God reveals himself in nature (general revelation) through the beauty and majesty of the world, this is only a small part of this revelation. God is not just satisfied that we know he exists; he wants us to know who he is. God not only reveals himself in nature but also through his Son, through his Word, through prayer and through others.

God does not just reveal himself through words, he reveals himself in actions.

Contrary to what some Christians may think, God is not vague, mysterious or shy about disclosing who he is. He not only tells us who he is, he shows us. His words and actions agree. When he acts, he explains what he is doing with an interpretive word. For example, God promises the Israelites that, "I will be your God and you shall be my people. " He demonstrated this in action when he delivered the Israelites from Egypt, "I am the Lord your God who brought you out of Egypt, out of the house of Bondage" (Exodus 20: 2) (ASV). The best example of God telling us and then showing us is Christ. God tells us he loves us and then sacrifices his son to prove it.

When it comes to the Bible I tell my clients, "In my opinion the Bible tells me two things; it tells me *who God is* and *who I am*." How I use this information (revelation) makes all the difference." In my opinion, everything God reveals to us is to be used for one purpose — to enhance our relationship with him. If we only read Scripture to understand God, and learn nothing new about ourselves, we have only read half the Bible.

For example the parable about the "prodigal son" not only tells us about a wayward youth it tells us about the love of a father. The story of the servant who buried his talent is as much about him as it is about the returning landlord. If we cannot see ourselves in the characters of Noah, Moses, the Pharaoh, Martha or Peter, then we have missed a bunch!

A meaningful relationship with God starts with a clear understanding of him. In 1952, B. J. Phillips wrote a book entitled, _Your God Is Too Small._ I read this book some thirty years ago in seminary and I use it with clients almost daily. The premise of this book is that we continually limit God by viewing him through our humanness, which skews our concept of him and limits his power. As Christians we have a tendency to restrict our spirituality by limiting what we think God can and will do.

We must be careful that our theology is not just our "psychology recycled." The problem lies in using our experiences in this world to shape and limit our concept of God. If we have trust issues with others, then this mistrust tends to be transferred to our concept of God. If we struggle with feelings of inadequacy and believe we are unacceptable, then we will have trouble accepting God's grace.

As a therapist I am aware that our theology begins to form long before we reach any age of accountability. As children our initial concept of God quite often is our father, mother, grandparent or caregiver. Children make decisions about love, acceptance and grace through the relationships at hand. Those children who have had positive experiences with these concepts find it easy to see love, acceptance and grace in Christianity. Those individuals who have not experienced these concepts in a healthy way tend to struggle spiritually.

If as children, we see life as being hard and fraught with peril and danger, then as adults, we will tend to see Christianity the same way. If our parental figures were abusive or threatening, then there is a chance that our concept of God will be based on fear. As adults we must be careful that our childhood experiences and environment do not continue to shape our concept of God. Paul cautions us about this in Romans 12:2, *"To not be fashioned according to this world: but be ye transformed by the renewing of your mind, and ye may prove what is the good and acceptable and perfect will of God"* (ASV).

If we believe that God can only love as I love, forgive as I forgive, and do what I can do, we have made him small. 1 Corinthians 13:12 says, *"We see through the glass darkly."* This limited view of our world is like traveling through Europe in a railroad boxcar and looking out through a knothole. While we would be able to say that we saw Europe, our description and experience would leave a lot to be desired.

All athletes want to be number one; they want to be the *best*. Christian athletes, on the other hand, want to be the *best they can be,* which means putting God first. Being the best in athletic terms means being better than all the rest. It is determined and achieved on the field of play and takes place at a particular moment. Being all you can be in spiritual terms means being equal with all the rest and is played out in life as a process. The former can be accomplished alone the latter cannot. Being the best is self-serving while being the best Christian means serving God.

One of the key principles of sports theology is that potential is tied to faith. Sport theology has no problem with the belief that individual athletes can learn techniques to improve performance. Sports theology just says that without God's revelation, human beings are limited in what they know in general. Revelation is about knowledge and when it comes to knowledge, God's pool is deeper than man's.

Through their relationship and faith in God, Christian athletes not only better understand the purpose of their athletic ability; they have a better understanding of life in general. They are better equipped as athletes, and most importantly, they are better equipped as individuals. Knowing God provides them with the foundation and direction they need to be all they can be.

As I mentioned earlier, the Bible not only tells us about God; it tells us about ourselves. I call this biblical revelation about mankind "spiritual anthropology." God does not only reveal himself in scripture, he tells us about us. In part, the Bible is a historical record of man's relationship with God. In the Old and New Testaments we see documentation of man's victories and failures, faith and doubt and strengths and weaknesses.

It is through this documentation of man's relationship with God that we see our value as individuals. In the fabric of this historical record we see that his love for us is awesome and his devotion to us is endless. To see ourselves through the eyes of God allows us to be transformed, to overcome the limitations put on us by the world.

Knowing that God is a loving God and that he values us unconditionally, frees us up from the negative messages we have received in the past and will receive in the future. We can only truly know who we are and reach our potential through full awareness of who God is. This is the power of sports theology, "Then you will know the truth, and the truth will set you free" (John 8:32) (NIV).

Athletes who realize (through revelation) who God is, and who they are in relationship to him, function on a different level when it comes to knowledge and insight. For example, let's compare psychological insight to spiritual insight. Sports psychology uses the term *peak experience* to refer to an activity in which athletes feel like they are at one of the highest points of their lives. They find the moment exciting, fulfilling, joyful and transcendent. They feel very focused, aware of all that is going on around them and are in harmony with their physical, emotional and/or intellectual capabilities.

The athlete who pursues peak experiences in the realm of sports psychology is looking for this to take place on the field or through performance. Christian athletes know that being called by Christ allows peak experiences to take place anywhere. They can have peak experiences in their marriages, as parents or by serving their community. Their game-day peak experience could come from sharing their testimony while giving an autograph — even though they played poorly.

Through the transformation of revelation, Christian athletes have peak experiences quite often. If peak experience means finding moments of excitement, fulfillment and joy then Christian athletes have an advantage. If the definition of peak experience says that individuals are focused and are in harmony with their physical, emotional and/or intellectual capabilities, what better way to achieve this than through revelation? Sports theology believes that real harmony cannot come from just knowing our human capabilities, it comes from understanding our spirituality.

Sports psychology also talks about *peak performance*. Peak performance refers to behavior and performance that exceeds what is normally anticipated. It describes a very high level of functioning, often times, brought on by peak experiences. This is the desire of any athlete, to increase their level of performance, to perform at a higher level and to exceed their own expectations.

Once again insight through revelation is more powerful. If all we have to go on is our own perceptions and experiences then all things are limited, but with God, "all things are possible"(Romans 8:28, Ephesians 4:13). The Christian athlete accepts and expects the spectacular when he or she allows God to work through them. These athletes know that God is miraculous, " *God also bearing witness with them, both by signs and wonders, and by manifold powers, and by gifts of the Holy Spirit, according to his own will"* (Hebrews 2:4) (ASV). Through the combination of God's revelation and relationship Christian athletes have opened the door for athletic potential and possibilities beyond earthly expectations.

One last comparison between human insight and spiritual insight can be seen in the psychological term *inner conflict*. Inner conflict refers to the "wrestling match" that takes place between our Id, Ego and Super-ego. When this conflict is resolved in a satisfying way, we feel good about ourselves. When the conflict goes unresolved, or ends in an unsatisfactory way, we may find ourselves carrying bad feelings with us for an extended period of time.

Simply put (an oversimplification to be exact), this means that our instinctive needs and desires (Id), fight against our parental or moral attitudes and conscience (Superego) and is mediated by who we are and reality (Ego). Although all of this takes place in different levels of consciousness, one thing is clear, it is all about us.

Sports theology agrees that there is an inner conflict but rather sees this "wrestling match" as being spiritual in nature. The New Testament constantly refers to this conflict as the battle between our flesh (sinful nature of man) and our spirit (image of God). Galatians 5:6 tells us, *"So I say, walk by the Spirit, and you will not gratify the desires of the sinful nature"* (NIV). This is the battle mentioned in James 4:1, *"What causes fights and quarrels among you? Don't they come from your desires that battle within you"* (NIV)?

The advantage of viewing this conflict as spiritual rather than purely psychological is two-fold. First, this conflict is not relegated to the sub-conscious. Through God's revelation in Scripture, and through the life of Christ, we can see this battle is demonstrated in real life terms and examples. The second advantage for the Christian athlete is that they do not have to fight this battle alone, " *I have been crucified with Christ and I no longer live, but Christ lives in me. The life I now live in the body, I live by faith in the Son of God, who loved me and gave himself for me"* (Galatians 2:20) (NIV).

Christian athletes are transformed through the revelation of who God is and who they are in relationship to him. This is what being "born again" is all about. They no longer are limited by their own concepts and understanding. By viewing themselves through the eyes of God, Christian athletes avail themselves to his power;

they are able to grow spiritually, emotionally and intellectually. They have increased their potential as athletes and as individuals. Bernhard Langer, two-time winner of the Masters, talks about how God's revelation has changed his life:

> *"My best year ever came in 1985 — my first year as a member of the U.S. Tour. Not only did I win the Masters — the biggest event of my career — I also won the Heritage Classic in Hilton Head, the Australian Masters, the Casio World Open in Japan, the Sun City Million Dollar event and two events in Europe. I won seven tournaments on five different continents, and was ranked number one in the world. I had a beautiful wife and had achieved everything I could ever have dreamed of. But something was missing.*
>
> *My priorities were golf, golf, and more golf, then myself, and finally a little time with my wife. Every now and then, I prayed. I went to church. But if my golf game was not good, my whole life was miserable, and I made everyone around me miserable.*
>
> *The week after I won the Masters, I was invited by a friend and fellow touring pro to come to the PGA Tour Bible Study. That night was the first time in my life that I heard that I needed to be "reborn." It didn't make any sense to me. Surely, at*

the age of 28, I could not be born again. So at the end of the study, I asked the teacher what he meant by "reborn." He opened the Bible and showed me John 3:3, which reads: "Truly, truly I say to you, unless one is born again, he cannot see the kingdom of God."

I thought I was a "pretty good Christian," but I'd never heard this before. He went on to explain what it meant in practical terms. I was amazed to realize that the only way to have eternal life is through Jesus Christ—that He died for our sins. And that it is not through our deeds or good behavior that one receives eternal life, because we can never live up to God's standard. We will always fall short.

I've seen tremendous changes in my life, my marriage, and my whole outlook. My priorities have changed. They're now where they should be: God first, family second, and then my career. I believe when your priorities are in the right place everything is managed better."

Revelation is about God revealing himself, helping us understand who we are and the relationship between the two. Through Christ and God's Word we receive "divine truth" that tells us that God loves us and that we need his forgiveness. We not only see that we are flawed, we see what we can be. It is through revelation, and only revelation, that we are able to see clearly. Through the power of revelation we are transformed into spiritual beings. Armed with God's truth and the Holy Spirit, Christian athletes no longer are limited by their own understanding and can achieve more than they ever could have alone. They are clear minded; they understand their purpose and most of all, they know God is behind them. Through revelation they have unlocked their potential as individuals and as athletes.

CHAPTER 8

The Spirit-Filled Life – Balance

As Christians we must always be conscious of the two opposing forces at work within us all — the spiritual nature of man and the sinful nature of fallen man. We may lose individual battles but ultimately, through the sacrifice of a victorious Christ, we will win the war.

I often recall what my high school baseball coach used to tell us during infield practice. He would hit us ground balls, then yell, "Make the ball play you, don't play the ball." What he meant by this advice was, as infielders, we should never try to guess where the ball was going to bounce and then try to get there. He wanted us to get in front of the ball, get set, and take what came. He told us that if we attempted to guess where the ball was going to bounce, we would be on our heels and often out of position. One approach was based on doubt and uncertainty while the other was based on confidence and faith. The point here is that if we do not have a firm foundation and our lives are not based on the fundamentals of our faith, then we are constantly off balance.

An insecure "life stance" causes anxiety and leads to self-doubt. Anything that replaces God as our foundation is subject to decay, erosion and eventual failure. In 1 Corinthians 3:11 we read, *"For no one can lay any foundation other than the one already laid, which is Jesus Christ"* (NIV). We are "citizens of God's kingdom" built on foundation of Christ, *"Built on the foundation of the apostles and prophets, with Christ Jesus himself as the chief cornerstone"* (Ephesians 2:20) (NIV). Jesus built the Church on Peter (*petros* – the rock) who identified Jesus as Lord and Savior. The Christian athlete is like the wise man who built his house on rock as opposed to sand (Matthew 7:24).

In any diagram of balance there is a fulcrum and a lever. The fulcrum is the base and the lever is the platform, which is being balanced. There are a few ways to achieve balance. First, balance is affected by the size of the fulcrum. If the fulcrum is pointed then positioning of objects on the lever is more critical. For example, it is harder to balance a basketball on one finger than it is in your hand. The fulcrum is the foundation upon which everything rests.

If our fulcrum in life is money, ego, prestige or anything that glorifies us then the fulcrum is pointed and sensitive to what is being balanced. Athletes who base their lives on performance, winning, or personal accolades have a pointed and tentative fulcrum (foundation) upon which to balance their lives. Christian athletes base their lives on the promises of Christ, according to the teachings of God's Word. Their fulcrum is wide and strong.

A second way to insure balance has to do with where objects are placed on the lever. The farther apart the opposing objects are from the fulcrum, the more fragile the balance. Christian athletes need to understand the farther they get from God, the more out of balance they become. If they keep God in the center of their lives, and live their lives in close proximity to him, things are more stable.

The third way to achieve balance is to be specific about the weight and placement of each object placed on the lever. Quite often I ask clients to describe what is weighing them down. Most times these individuals cannot even list the things that are on their "lever," much less give value of weight to each object. To make things worse, many times they are carrying things that don't even belong to them.

Spiritual minded athletes know what is important in life and can value things appropriately. They are able to prioritize the things they carry and attempt to balance. They live their lives to glorify God and nothing becomes more important than that; small things that should not be on their lever do not distract them. They do not value personal achievement over glorifying God, winning over witnessing or the expectations of others over the call of Jesus Christ.

When things begin to get out of balance the lever begins to tilt. Eventually the lever tilts to the point that everything slides to the bottom of a severe incline. This is what it feels like to be out of balance. We have all had times when we felt that things were piling up and life was an "uphill climb." We have either lost our center, misjudged the weight of things or have taken on too much. We have lost our balance.

Athletes who put their faith and value in statistics or winning and losing, often find themselves at the bottom of this incline covered up with doubt, frustration and hopelessness. They feel like the world has come crashing down on them and they begin to question their value and ability. In most cases they have just simply lost their balance. They have built their lives on sand and have valued the wrong things.

Any book about physical fitness/health or sports psychology talks about the importance of balance: diet; training, recovery, emotions and thoughts during competition. Other disciplines talk about the importance of balancing psychological conditioning and physical skills or the need for athletes to have a balanced lifestyle. There are even *neurofeedback* studies that attempt to improve physical balance. No matter how you view balance, it is important to athletes.

When it comes to athletic performance, these are all legitimate and helpful uses of the term balance. One of Webster's main definitions of balance *refers to stability that comes from an even distribution of weight.* Athletes are most familiar with this usage of balance. They know that they cannot perform if they are physically off balance. Balance in this case means a steady foundation upon which physical skills can be accurately performed. The offensive tackle or gymnast will tell you how bad things go when they attempt to perform off-balance.

Another use of the word balance refers *to the weight or force of one side to another.* This usage means the ability to keep things on an even keel. In life, we all know what it is like to attempt to balance everything as not to let one thing out-weigh another. How many times have we felt like we are participants in a "balancing act?" In this sense it does not really matter if as athletes we are trying to balance training and recovery, emotions and thoughts or expectations and performance: the goal is equality in importance and value.

Balance can also be used in reference to *future outcome*, to talk about the importance of an event in the future. Many times stress and anxiety comes from the combination of the importance we put on an event and the fear of not knowing how things will turn out. This is what is meant when someone says, "Our survival hangs in the balance." As we have mentioned throughout this book, Christian athletes never see anything in this world as more important than their relationship with Christ, which is never challenged by the events of the day. God's love and support is constant.

The last usage for balance here is when it refers to the *final equation* or the *unknown*. Balance here means the end result or how things will turn out. This is true in accounting, in competition and in life. We tend to fret about what is going to happen next or spend time trying to control or prepare for the unknown. This attempt to predict or control the future inevitably ties us to this world and consumes the majority of our waking time and energy.

Trying to predict what is going to happen next in life is as futile as trying to predict where a baseball is going to bounce. The end result is that we tend to live our lives out of balance and on our heels. In both cases, the only thing we can control is how we position ourselves as life comes at us. It is true that we cannot control the world but we can choose how to live in it. For the Christian athlete control is replaced by grace, "...*my grace is sufficient for thee: for (my) power is made perfect in weakness. Most gladly therefore will I rather glory in my weaknesses, that the power of Christ may rest upon me*" (2 Corinthians 12:9) (RSV).

Balance is a key part of living the Christian life. We all must balance the two opposing natures of man, which are the fallen nature (flesh) and the image of God in us all. Being made in the image of God means that we are spiritual by nature. The farther we get from our spiritual nature the more off balance we become. Paul tells us in Romans 8:12-13,

> "*Therefore, brothers and sisters, we have an obligation – but it is not to the sinful nature, to live according to it. For if you*

> *live according to the flesh, you will die;*
> *but if by the Spirit you put to death the*
> *misdeeds of the body, you will live"*
> *(NIV).*

The Greek word for flesh here is *sarx*, which means: *the body as opposed to the soul, or as the symbol of what is external, or human nature, a human being.*

To tell you the truth, growing up I always thought that "flesh" only referred to sins related to lust. That concept was somewhat easier to keep a handle on. As one looks at the Biblical usage of flesh, it becomes evident that the meaning here is much broader. The New Testament usage of flesh relates to all things done out of our humanness rather than out of Spirit. Defining flesh in this way has tremendous ramifications as to how we view and live our lives.

This definition of flesh describes the nature of fallen man (Chapter 2). The interaction between flesh and Spirit describes the constant battle we fight throughout our Christian lives (Chapter 7). This battle is described as, law versus grace, the world versus the kingdom of God, sin versus justification, self-righteousness versus meekness, doubt versus faith, self versus service and so on.

What is important about this definition is that it tells us that we are constantly prone to act out of our human nature (flesh), which leads to self-centeredness, resulting in our focusing on what we want and think we need. Adam's self-centeredness caused the problem in the garden and is the same mistake we continually make today. If we live our lives out of our humanness, we cannot achieve the spiritual life we desire.

Left to our own devices we cannot achieve the true happiness, peace and joy that allow us to experience the fullness of God's love. In Galatians 2:20 Paul tells us: "*I have been crucified with Christ; and it is no longer I that live, but Christ living in me: and that (life) which I now live in the flesh I live in faith, (the faith) which is in the Son of God, who loved me, and gave himself up for me*" (ASV).

The reason this passage is so important to the Christian life is that it tells me that as long as I am the center of my life then there is no place for Christ. Unchecked, we have a tendency to live in this world, falling prey to our humanness which brings with it the trials and tribulations of materialism, greed, insecurity, pettiness, stress, depression, etc. (pretty much everything listed in Galatians 5:19-21).

Many times we do not even realize that we have seized control of our own lives and are closed to God. We are not bad people: we don't intend to hinder our relationship with God. This natural but subtle shift from God to "self" changes everything. Self-centered, self-adsorbed individuals have become the center of their lives — they have become the fulcrum.

How significant is this subtle change from Christ-centered to flesh-centered? The change can be huge. In Matthew 22:36-40, Christ tells us that the two greatest commandments are, "*to love God with all our heart and soul and love our neighbor as our-selves*" (ASV). Both of these commandments require that we think of another before ourselves, a task we, as self-centered individuals, often fail to do. Obedience here is the difference between serving ourselves and serving Christ.

The self-centered Christian has fallen into the trap of trying to work out his or her own happiness, or, as I like to say, his or her own salvation Not only does this self-imposed edification cause problems in our relationship with God, it also fails to get us what we want in the here and now.   If we are going to be our own deity, then we had better have all the answers. We had better have a clear view of others as well as ourselves. If we are going to be god, then we must always know what is best for us and how to obtain these things. Obviously this attempt to deify self is not only folly, it is down right dangerous.

Self-deified individuals must never sleep. They are in charge and must control their world. Self-reliant individuals are cursed with a never-ending battle to make themselves feel good, valuable, and powerful. When such individuals become the center of their own belief system, doubt and failure cannot be tolerated. Self-doubt and fear of failure threaten the foundation of their world. This system will, of course, fail to provide a sense of value, sense of hope and fulfillment. In fact, many times this futile attempt to control one's life only causes frustration and bitterness. The attempt to find happiness through our own power will end badly. Worshipping ourselves only adds pressure, which prevents us from living the Spirit-filled life we desire (Matthew 13:22).

Not only is self-edification hard on the individual in his or her personal life, it negatively affects their relationships. Individuals, who attempt to earn their own value or love, have trouble in relationships at work, in friendships and in marriage. It is one thing for people to go through the day trying to prove that they are loved as opposed to going through the day knowing they are loved. Individuals who doubt they are loveable spend most of their time trying to prove it. This attempt in itself sets up interactions and actions that are once again self-centered. The insecure person does not have time to care for the needs of others.

Spiritual living means that we are always conscious of the need to balance the two opposing forces at work within us all — the spiritual nature of man and the sinful nature of fallen man. Being engaged in this religious struggle is spiritual living. Acknowledging our brokenness and our constant need for Christ is all we are called to do. We may lose individual battles but ultimately, through the sacrifice of a victorious Christ, we will win the war.

Balance is not about perfection; it is about keeping our eyes on Christ no matter what. Paul tells us in Philippians 3:12, *"Not that I have already obtained, or am already made perfect: but I press on...."* (ASV). What this verse says to me is that salvation is not tied to what I accomplish in this world on my own. Salvation and personal value do not come from personal perfection. Paul goes on to say that even though perfection is not possible, he continues to pursue it as "the high calling of God in Jesus Christ." Living the spirit-filled life is not about perfection; it is about pursuit and direction. The point is, that although some sort of "spiritual utopia" may never be reached, the pursuit of it can be constant.

What does all this have to do with athletic performance? It has a lot. If you recall, sports theology is built on the premise that athletic ability is a gift from God. The goal of the athletes is to make sure that they do not hinder this gift. When it comes to maximizing God's gifts, being off balance is a big distraction. Sports theology is all about clearing away those things that get between God and us. It is about using God as our focus, or in this case, our fulcrum.

Athletes who perform spiritually appreciate the need for balance like any other athlete. These athletes just approach balance from a different perspective. They acquire balance through their relationship with God. Living the spirit-filled life allows athletes to maintain equilibrium, to balance all aspects of their lives and embrace the unknown.

In chapter 2 we talked about how pride, fear and control can distract athletes from freely demonstrating the gifts God has given them. When we talk about living in balance we are also talking about managing the empirical, practical day-to-day things in life. Athletes do not perform or live in a vacuum. We talked earlier about how athletes at the highest level get a double dose of pressure. They perform their profession under the microscope of the press and in front of thousands, and sometimes, millions. This is also true when it comes to balancing all the things that come with fame or the spotlight.

If you talk to any professional athlete you will find that they struggle with balancing all that comes with "the life style." They must practice, play, give interviews, manage their career, make personal appearances and then be husbands/wives and parents. Although this is a lot to manage, this is not where most professional athletes loose the battle of balance. Those high profile athletes who are honest with themselves and others will tell you that the problem is the temptations that come with notoriety in sports.

One professional athlete (who will remain nameless) told me that the real danger comes from the "behind the scenes" activities of professional sports. Most pro-athletes don't talk about the drugs, alcohol, sex and money that come with the fame and notoriety. Perhaps it is the amount of time required or the continual pressure put on these athletes, but either way, they are at risk of losing their balance. It would be easy to judge athletes who fall prey to these temptations but the majority of us will never know what it is like to walk in their shoes. I am not sure that we would fare much better, *"Watch and pray so that you will not fall into temptation. The spirit is willing, but the flesh is weak"* (Matthew 26:41)(NIV).

Christian athletes are human too and are at risk of being seduced by the temptations of this life style. As we have mentioned earlier, Christian athletes are aware that perfection is unobtainable and that they may spiritually stumble. The benefit of knowing Christ allows them the opportunity of confession, forgiveness and restoration. All of which allows them to live and perform with a sense of freedom.

They have two advantages when it comes to "being balanced". First of all, Scripture warns them about putting anything before their relationship with God. They are familiar with 1 Timothy 6:9, *"Those who want to get rich fall into temptation and a trap and into many foolish and harmful desires that plunge people into ruin and destruction"*(NIV). These athletes know that they will be tested by the world and are aware of the temptations that threaten their calling, *"Blessed are those who persevere under trial, because when they have stood the test, they will receive the crown of life that God has promised to those who love him* (James 1:12)(NIV).

The second reason Christian athletes remain balanced is that they stand firmly on the foundation of Christ. By living the spirit-filled life these athletes are protected or insulated from the power of temptation,

> *"Wherefore take up the whole armor of God, that ye may be able to withstand in the evil day, and, having done all, to stand. Stand therefore, having girded your loins with truth, and having put on the breastplate of righteousness, and having shod your feet with the preparation of the gospel of peace; withal taking up the shield of faith, wherewith ye shall be able to quench all the fiery darts of the evil (one). And take the helmet of salvation, and the sword of the Spirit, which is the word of God"* (Ephesians 6:13-17) (ASV).

Being balanced spiritually means living our lives based on the love of God and the promises of Christ. It is on this spiritual foundation that everything is weighed, placed and valued. Athletes who are grounded by faith are better equipped to balance their lives. With God as their fulcrum they are able to prioritize their lives and balance the pressure of athletics and everyday life. They are able to overcome the desires of the flesh and embrace their spiritual nature. They are able to focus on performance because they have less on their plate. They are not carrying guilt, shame, and fear with them to the playing field. Their lives are in balance.

CHAPTER 9

The Body of Christ – Team

Through God's Word and the life of Christ we see the power in teamwork. There is equal value put on the importance of the individual and the team — one is never disconnected from the other.

Most athletes perform as members of a team. Personal performance is as important in team sports as it is in individual sports, but as a member of a team the athlete must perform in concert with others to be successful. In most studies on team psychology the term *cohesion* is used to describe a desired bond between team members. Cohesion is commonly broken into two types, *task cohesion* and *social cohesion*. Task cohesion refers to the way team members work with each other to successfully complete a task. A group is given an overall team goal, which is accepted and valued by all team members. Social cohesion involves personal relationships within the group and relies on individuals enjoying social activities together.

There is no research that proves cohesion increases the odds of winning. There have been teams in which players did not get along, yet they still won championships. That is to say that a team can win with task cohesion (working together to accomplish a task) without social cohesion (social activities and relationships). I would venture to guess (research or not) that a team with both is harder to beat.

If you talk to coaches they will tell you that teamwork is a key to success. When you hear terms like "chemistry" or "coming together" it usually means that a team has played with a common identity and purpose. Babe Ruth once said, "*The way a team plays as a whole determines its success. You may have the greatest bunch of individual stars in the world, but if they don't play together, the club won't be worth a dime.*" For a team to be successful athletes must be willing to see beyond themselves. As Paul (Bear) Bryant has said, *"In order to have a winner, the team must have a feeling of unity; every player must put the team first - ahead of personal glory."*

We have all seen the case of a superb athlete being traded from team to team due to his inability to "fit in." We also know that any team that relies on one player to succeed usually falls short. No matter what coaches say on television, a team with one *great* player does not concern them as much as a team with five or ten *good* players playing together. Knute Rockne once said, *"The secret is to work less as individuals and more as a team. As a coach, I play not my eleven best, but my best eleven."* I have been told that, the individual is important to the team unless the individual becomes more important than the team itself.

I once asked an NFL player if he missed the camaraderie of his teammates in the off-season. He told me that there was not much camaraderie to miss. He talked about how different things were in pro football as compared to what they were like in college. At the pro-level everyone did their own thing. Groups or cliques were formed by positions: defense with defense, offense with offense, running backs with running backs and so on. Relationships were formed by common interest in nightlife routines and extra-curricular activities. He told me that the player in the next locker did not talk to him for the first year because he was a rookie. In his view the goal was to get the big money or make SportsCenter highlights on ESPN. In his view, "Football had become a business. It was no longer a team but individuals showing up for work."

The bottom line is that a group of highly tuned athletes "does not a team make." But if you can find a skilled athlete who understands the power of teamwork, then you have something special. Michael Jordan makes this point when he says,

> *"There are plenty of teams in every sport that have great players and never win titles. Most of the time, those players aren't willing to sacrifice for the greater good of the team. The funny thing is, in the end, their unwillingness to sacrifice only makes individual goals more difficult to achieve...If you think and achieve as a team, the individual accolades will take care of themselves. Talent wins games, but teamwork and intelligence win championships."*

Christian athletes are more prone to be team players because they understand the two basic elements of the team concept, which are being less focused on themselves and knowing what it is like to be part of something greater. They understand what it means to be part of a team from being part of the body of Christ.

In the New Testament there are three uses for the term "body of Christ." It is used to refer to the human form of God, to represent God's sacrifice in communion and to represent fellowship among believers (the universal church). In all three of these cases the word "body" means more than the literal human anatomy. In each case "the body of Christ" encourages us to become more than our physical form and become part of something greater. In these three uses of the body of Christ we find the foundation of the team concept.

The first meaning of the body of Christ relates to the embodiment of God in Jesus Christ. This is an important concept for two reasons. First, through Christ, God communicates his love for us in a way that we can understand — in human form, *"The Word became flesh and made his dwelling among us. We have seen his glory, the glory of the one and only Son, who came from the Father, full of grace and truth"* (John 1:4) (NIV). Secondly, through Christ's humanness, we have a model of what a relationship with God can be like. This is expressed in Galatians 2:20,

> *"I have been crucified with Christ; and it is no longer I that live, but Christ living in me: and that (life) which I now live in the flesh I live in faith, (the faith) which is in the Son of God, who loved me, and gave himself up for me." (ASV)*

Through the model of Christ, Christian athletes can learn a lot about God and teamwork. No matter what the situation Jesus found himself in, he never lost touch with the Father. His life was based not on himself but on the goals and desires of God. Jesus was a high profile personality (much like athletes of today) who could have easily been seduced by fame and the temptations of the material world (Matthew 4:1-10). It was because of Jesus' ability to live his life from God's perspective that gave him strength and value. God's love was sufficient.

The same is true for Christian athletes. Being part of the body of Christ allows them to play fulfilled by God's love. They are able to see past their own importance because they are content, and complete and have nothing to prove. They can focus on the goals of another because Jesus demonstrated this on a grander scale. The Christian athlete is free from the need of temporal approval or the accolades from individual performance. Spiritually, these athletes are satisfied by God's love and have plenty to give to the team. Lance Berkman of the Houston Astros, talks about being spiritually content and a team player when he says,

> *"Living the Christian life is also challenging but for different reasons. The same desire to do well exists - to live a consistent life that honors and pleases the Lord. The big difference is that God isn't evaluating my actions and basing His love on how well I "perform". His love for me is unconditional. Even when I mess up He doesn't threaten to trade me off His team."*

The body of Christ is also used to represent the sacrifice of Christ. At the "last supper," Jesus used the analogy of body as bread, blood as wine to symbolize our salvation in his sacrifice. At the last supper Jesus said,

> *"And as they were eating, he took bread, and when he had blessed it, he broke it,*

and gave to them, and said, Take ye: this is my body. And he took a cup, and when he had given thanks, he gave to them: and they all drank of it. And he said unto them, this is my blood of the covenant, which is poured out for many" (Mark 14: 22-24) (ASV).

Someone once said that, "teamwork is defined as a group of people quietly engaged in self-sacrifice." Larry Bird was quoted to say, "It doesn't matter who scores the points, it's who can get the ball to the scorer." Mia Hamm describes what team means to her when she says, "I am a member of a team, and I rely on the team, I defer to it and sacrifice for it, because the team, not the individual, is the ultimate champion." Taking these quotes into consideration, I would say that one of the characteristics of a team player is personal sacrifice.

It is easy to take the punishment and training if on game-day you can carry the ball into the end zone with 70,000 fans applauding your accomplishment. I respect the offensive tackle who does not see the touchdown because his is under the 300-pound linebacker he just blocked to spring the running back. This is a demonstration of self- sacrifice in team sports. The true team player will do what he or she has to do for the greater good of the team.

Those athletes who perform theologically need look no further than Jesus Christ to find a role model for self-sacrifice. Through Jesus we see the ultimate example of giving up self for the greater good. Christian athletes are aware that who they are and what they do is not where the focus is. As members of the body of Christ they are not put off by the concept of performing for a greater purpose. They can sacrifice themselves for the team because Christ sacrificed himself for them. Dave Johnson, Olympic Medalist Decathlon, says it best when he says,

> *"I'm always trying to give 100 percent to God - anything less would be unacceptable as far as Christ is concerned. He gave 100 percent of Himself for us - He died for us! If He had given anything else we would fall well short of reaching God."*

Vince Lombardi once said, " *Football is like life — it requires perseverance, self-denial, hard work, sacrifice, dedication and respect for authority.*" The same thing could be said to describe Christ.

The sacrifice of the human Jesus is theologically significant for two reasons. First, it is unique to Christianity that God becomes flesh. In no other religion does God become one of us. It is a powerful demonstration of God's love to put himself in human form to reach mankind. Secondly, it is through the human form of Jesus that salvation takes place.

We are not accepted by God due to our own deeds or accomplishments but are saved by being transformed into "brothers and sisters" of Christ. Through Christ we are deemed righteous, *"He is the atoning sacrifice for our sins, and not only for ours but also for the sins of the whole world* (1 John 2:2) (NIV). In this sense the "body of Christ" is not only an important theological term, it represents the pivotal point in God's plan for our salvation and the future of mankind. Once again we must look beyond ourselves,

> *"For what the law was powerless to do because it was weakened by the sinful nature, God did by sending his own Son in the likeness of sinful humanity to be a sin offering. And so he condemned sin in human flesh" (Romans 8:3) (NIV).*

Salvation is not something we can earn on our own; it only comes from identifying with Christ.

In these first two meanings of the body of Christ we can see the importance of living outside of ourselves. This is even more evident in the third meaning, which refers to the universal church. In The New Testament the Greek word for church is *ekklesia*, which is translated to mean: *The body of Christ or fellowship of believers on earth or saints in heaven.* As Christians we are not called or encouraged to work alone. As followers (body) of Christ we are members of the "fellowship of believers," part of a community.

It is through our ability to embrace the fellowship of others that we gain acceptance, encouragement and help,

> *"Think of ways to encourage one another to outbursts of love and good deeds. Not giving up meeting together, as some are in the habit of doing, but encouraging*

one another – and all the more as you see the day approaching" (Hebrews 10:24-25) (NIV).

It is through community that great things can be accomplished. As we all know, there is strength in numbers, *"Though one may be overpowered, two can defend themselves. A chord of three strands is not quickly broken"* (Ecclesiastes 4:12). It is through the universal church that the great commission will be met. Through the body of Christ God takes advantage of the individual skills of his followers to reach the world with the "good news."

To embrace the concept of community, or fellowship with others, does not diminish the importance of the individual. It is not about feeling less valuable about who we are, but rather is about appreciating the value of others. The concept of Christian fellowship, or being part of the body of Christ, is about using our individual skills for a greater purpose, to become part of something bigger. Paul talks about the selfless attitude that comes with being part of the body of Christ in Philippians 2:2-5,

"Then make me truly happy by agreeing wholeheartedly with each other, loving one another, and working together with one heart and purpose. Don't be selfish; don't live to make a good impression on others. Be humble, thinking of others as better than yourself. Don't think only about your own affairs, but be interested

in others and what they are doing. Your attitude should be the same that Christ Jesus had"(Philippians 2:2-5)(NLT).

The concept of the universal church applies itself best to the sports psychology term of social cohesion. The word "Christian" (khristianos) originated in the first century in Antioch to represent the "disciples of Christ." The New Testament uses the body of Christ to represent the fellowship of believers who were always being persecuted by Rome. To be identified as a Christian, was to be at risk. Early Christians knew what it was like to work as a team, not only for worship, but also for protection.

In the term "body of Christ" we see that the individual is valued as part of the whole, *"Now all of you together are Christ's body, and each one of you is a separate and necessary part of it"*(1 Corinthians 12:27) (NLT). Webster defines fellowship as, *a company of equals or friends.* This is probably the most powerful ingredient in the team concept. A team must work together; they must have a mutual respect and trust for one another. In this sense, the body of Christ is the ultimate model for equality and demonstrates the importance of diversity. In 1 Corinthians 12:13-20 we find one of the best descriptions of the team concept:

"For in one Spirit were we all baptized into one body, whether Jews or Greeks, whether bond or free; and were all made to drink of one Spirit. For the body is not

one member, but many. If the foot shall say, because I am not the hand, I am not of the body; it is not therefore not of the body. And if the ear shall say, because I am not the eye, I am not of the body; it is not therefore not of the body. If the whole body were an eye, where would be the hearing? If the whole were hearing, where is the smelling? But now hath God set the members each one of them in the body, even as it pleased him. And if they were all one member, where were the body? But now they are many members, but one body."(ASV)

The good thing about performing as part of the body of Christ is that it even brings the team concept to athletes who play individual sports. The Christian professional tennis player or golfer can take advantage of the team dynamic as a member of the body of Christ. God never sees an individual's performance or career as being isolated or unimportant. As Christians we all perform for the same God and goal, to glorify him. Individual athletes are empowered by God; they sacrifice themselves to glorify him and are part of the greatest team in the world.

In my opinion there is no better model for team sports than the term "body of Christ" found in the New Testament. Within this term we see the value in sacrifice, community, the individual and appreciation for diversity. Through God's Word and the life of Christ we see the power in teamwork. There is equal value put on the importance of the individual and the team — one is never disconnected from the other. Through the concept of the universal church we see the support and power that comes from playing as a team.

CHAPTER 10

Testify –
Self-Actualization

If sports were really about statistics then games would not need to be played. Athletes who tie their ability or value to "the stats" are asking for trouble. Many people will say, "The stats don't lie." I say statistics are like fishermen, "The truth is not in them."

The biggest deterrent to living a spirit-filled life is that most of us do not believe what we say we believe. That may sound hard, but it is true. Becoming a Christian is only the first step in the process of living the Christian life. Granted, accepting Christ and being assured of our salvation is paramount but the process does not stop there. In fact, it has just begun. Now I am not saying that just because a Christian is not living the abundant life, he or she is not a real Christian. But, I am saying, that a Christian who is not living a full spiritual life is underachieving.

The definition of self-actualization is: *to fully realize one's potential.* The word "realize" here does not just mean to understand something but to bring it into *concrete existence.* Self-actualization is not about conception; it is about performance. It is about being all you can be and doing the best you can do. This is the goal of sports psychology — that athletes will perform to the best of their ability. In sports psychology maximum performance is the goal. In sports theology maximum performance is not the goal but rather the by-product of reaching our potential as Christians. In sports theology the athlete does the best he or she can do because they are being the best they can be.

As Christians, performance is not the "sum of our parts" but rather is an "out cropping" of the gifts given to us by God — it is our calling. Rick Warren makes this point in book, *The Purpose Driven Life,*

"You were made by God for God — and until you understand that, life will never

> *make sense. It is only in God that we dis-*
> *cover our origin, our identity, our mean-*
> *ing, our purpose, our significance and*
> *our destiny. Every other path leads to a*
> *dead end."*

Athletic ability, like all gifts from God, makes us who we are and shows others who we serve. For Christian athletes, performance is not just an opportunity to glorify them; it is a chance to testify that Jesus Christ is Lord.

We have all heard the saying, "Don't just talk the talk – you need to walk the walk." As Christians we are called to do both. We are called "to testify." The word testify appears to be a simple word or concept but it is powerful and vital when it comes to living the Christian life. The word testify means living out what we believe, it is the foundation of our conviction and empowers our calling of Christ. Acts 20:24 says, *"But I hold not my life of any account as dear unto myself, so that I may accomplish my course, and the ministry which I received from the Lord Jesus, to testify the gospel of the grace of God"* (ASV). In this verse we see that our purpose is not to glorify ourselves: we are here to testify on God's behalf.

The Greek word for testify in Acts 20:24 is *dia-marturomai,* which means, *to attest or profess earnestly, or to be charged, testify (unto), witness.* Webster defines the verb *to testify* to mean: *1 a: to make a statement based on personal knowledge or belief: bear witness b: to serve as evidence or proof 2: to express a personal conviction 3: to make a solemn declaration under oath for the purpose of establishing a fact (as in a court).*

Through these two definitions we can begin to see how important the word testify is. I do not want to get too wordy or make this a vocabulary lesson, but we need to break this down a bit.

One of the definitions of "to testify" means *to make a statement based on personal knowledge or belief: to bear witness or attest to.* In this sense testify means to attest that something is true. It is a tangible proof of tribute; it is a *testament* of fact. As in all theological truth, God is first to demonstrate what he wants us to do. The Bible is God's testament (old and new) of his love for us. In Scripture God not only tells us about this love for us, it is a record of how he has demonstrated this love. This testament or covenant is described in Hebrews 9:15,

> *"For this reason Christ is the mediator of a new covenant, that those who are called may receive the promised eternal inheritance – now that he has died as a ransom to set them free from the sins committed under the first covenant"* (NIV).

To bear witness means that we not only *say* what we believe, we *act* on what we believe.

Living the Christian life in a spiritually-filled manner, not only strengthens our relationship with God; it also enables us to serve him better. It is through the powerful combination of God's grace and our faith that our lives become a testament to God in this world.

Through the Holy Spirit each one of us has the ability to use our lives as a witness to the power of Christ.

Spiritually–based athletes know that their athletic ability is from God and develop this gift and perform as a testament to him. This view of performance makes a big difference when it comes to handling the pressure of competition. For the Christian athlete the outcome of a competition is not as important as the act of competing in it. In their view, just performing is a blessing and gives them the opportunity to "bear witness."

By acknowledging God's gifts, and using these gifts for his purpose, Christian athletes solidify the covenant between God and themselves. As we have said, in the Old and New Testaments we find God's words and actions that define his part of this covenant. Athletes who performs spiritually are not only acknowledging this covenant, they are fulfilling their part of it. Albert Pujols of the St. Louis Cardinals says it this way, *".... At the end of the day as long as I glorify him and those 45,000 people know who I represent, every time I step out on the field, that's what it's about. It's about representing God."*

To testify also means to serve as evidence of proof. In a word, this means to give *testimony*. In a court of law this means, "to provide first hand authentication of fact." It means the same thing theologically. It is through our testimony, experiences past and present, that our devotion to God is proven. Exodus 23:2 tells us, *"Do not follow the crowd in doing wrong. When you give testimony in a lawsuit, do not pervert justice by siding with the crowd"*(NIV). To misrepresent the truth in a court of law is perjury; to say we are Christians and not live it is sin.

As we have said, "It is through our testimony, experiences past and present, that our devotion to God is proven." This statement helps Christian athletes to put individual events and performances in perspective. It enables them to understand that glorifying God is a life long process. This statement also tells them that testimony is not limited to what is said, it must be a combination of word and deed. In athletic terms, testimony is about a career not an individual game. Once again, this is not about if you win or lose; it is how you play the game. But testimony encompasses more than just how an athlete performs. Christian athletes live their lives based on the principles of Christ and approach performance like everything else: with humility, self-sacrifice and devotion to God.

We have already talked about the fact that those individuals at the top of their sport live under a microscope. Their personal and professional lives are often exposed for all to see. Quite often we hear a particular athlete say that he or she resents being called a "role model" just because they are successful. They say that it is unfair to be put in this situation and that they never volunteered for such responsibility. Two things come to my mind when I hear this. First, these athletes are probably not living the kind of lives they are proud of, and secondly, Christian athletes never say this.

Spiritual athletes see notoriety as the opportunity to glorify God. They see their athletic ability and accomplishments as a platform to tell others where their real strength and purpose comes from. Christian athletes do no fear others knowing how they live their lives or what they do off the field. They are fully aware that their testimony comes from all they do and not just how they perform. These athletes approach individual competition as part of the whole, not something that defines them in a moment or a single event. They view performance like they do anything else — just another chance to share their testimony.

Christ tells us that the two greatest commandments are, *"To Love the Lord your God with all your heart and with all your soul and with all your strength and with all your mind and love your neighbor as yourself"* (Luke 10:27) (NIV). This is the goal of the Christian athlete and is the foundation of their testimony. Self-actualization comes from being like Christ not from athletic performance. Excellence in athletic performance comes from meeting our potential as followers of Christ. How we approach performance defines us, we are not defined by the performance itself. Excellence comes from 1 Peter 4:10, which says, *"Each of you should use whatever gift you have received to serve others, as faithful stewards of God's grace in its various forms"* (NIV). As Christians we perform to the best of our ability because of who we <u>are</u>, not to <u>become</u> someone.

To testify also means to *profess*. To profess means *to declare or admit openly and freely, in words or appearance*. It has been said that in personal interactions we rely 30% on verbal communication and 70% on non-verbal. In inter-personal communication, trust and credibility comes when the non-verbal and verbal match.

This is just one example of what we do is more important than what we say. The consistency of word and deed fuels evangelism and gives our profession of faith authority. Unity between faith and action is the power behind the ministry of Jesus, the disciples and you and me. As Christians, our words, our hearts and our actions need to profess the same thing, *".... the word is near you; it is in your mouth and in your heart," that is, the message concerning faith that we proclaim*"(Romans 10:8) (NIV).

Theologically, the word testify can also mean being put to the *test*. Job's test (Job 2:3) was the basis of his testimony; his ultimate faithfulness was a testament to God. We are told in James 1:12, *"Blessed are those who persevere under trial, because when they have stood the test, they will receive the crown of life that God has promised to those who love him"* (NIV). Living our lives theologically changes the way we view personal crises in life. Hard times are viewed as opportunities rather than pitfalls or punishment.

In 1 Peter 1:6-7 we are told,

> *"There is wonderful joy ahead, even though it is necessary for you to endure many trials for a while. These trials are only to test your faith, to show that it is strong and pure. It is being tested as fire tests and purifies gold — and your faith is far more precious to God than mere gold. So if your faith remains strong after being tried by fiery trials, it will bring*

*you much praise and glory and honor on
the day when Jesus Christ is revealed to
the whole world" (NLT).*

In this verse we see the two spiritual benefits of being tested. First, being tested allows us to strengthen our faith. Trials and tribulations provide us with the opportunity to rely of the promises of Christ to overcome problems that may occur. In times of crises we can not only discover the weaknesses of our faith, we have the opportunity to strengthen it. This brings a different interpretation to the meaning of "trial and error." The Christian life is just that — the process of evaluation and growth.

The second spiritual benefit of being tested is that it gives us the opportunity to glorify God. I have told clients often that what has happened or whatever they have done, is not as important as what they do next. How we handle ourselves in the middle of crisis, or when we stumble, is a strong statement about our faith. Glorifying God often comes when things are tough. Spiritually, this is where the "rubber meets the road."

To testify also means to be tested. In Chapter One we talked about the fact that athletes have to deal with immediate feedback about success or failure. It they miss a tackle, boot a ground ball or get passed on the last lap, failure is hard to deny. Athletes at the highest level will tell you that pressure comes from constantly being tested, physically, mentally and emotionally. The nature of sports is that these "pass/ fail" scenarios take place constantly; play by play and throughout a season.

Professional athletes are constantly being graded. They live and die by statistics such as batting averages, money lists, fairways hit and shooting percentages. There is real danger in living by statistics. Most coaches will tell you that what a team looks like on paper is not often the team they meet on the field. If sports were really about statistics then games would not need to be played. Athletes who tie their ability or value to "the stats" are asking for trouble. Athletes create statistics; statistics do not create athletes. Many people will say, "The stats don't lie." I say statistics are like fishermen, "The truth is not in them."

It is easy to see how athletes can become fatigued or loose confidence in this immediate pass/fail or statistical environment. One of the biggest advantages of sports theology comes into play here, about being tested. The Christian athlete lives with the same pressure to perform and is challenged and graded like everyone else. They view the whole process of being tested from a greater perspective. The difference is in their interpretation of *who* is testing them and *why* they are being tested. Christian athletes do not see the opposing lineman, point guard or goalie as the real test. They do not see each test as an indicator of their value.

Where does the test come from? Most athletes will tell you that real pressure comes from within — it is self-imposed. Christian athletes know this from Galatians 6:4, which says, " *Each of you should test your own actions. Then you can take pride in yourself, without comparing yourself to somebody else*" (NIV). Because Christians have Christ as their model they know what is right and how to live their lives. They desire to be more like him and embrace being tested so they can glorify God through spiritual living. These athletes set their own standards, which demonstrate their love and personal accountability to God.

This self-imposed desire to glorify God does not only bring athletes the pride mentioned in Galatians 6:4; it diminishes the pressure that comes with performance. To view any test as an opportunity rather than potential failure, is a powerful asset for the athlete. By setting their own standards, athletes are free from the opinions and values of others and can tie self-actualization to their relationship with God. Once athletes embrace the fact that the real pressure is internal (in their control) they can focus on *what* is being tested and not distracted by *who* is doing the testing.

The question then becomes why are we being tested? As Christians we are tested for one reason and one reason only — to strengthen our faith. Most of us have a negative view of the word *test*. This distaste for the word test probably originated from all those years in school where tests equaled grades, grades equaled parental response and their response could affect freedom or restriction. Simply put, this sets up the connection between being tested and passing or failing. This of course is a perversion of the concept of testing. Students are tested to see where they fall short of the knowledge needed. It is a positive exercise that defines areas in which to improve. How do we know if we have mastered something if we are never tested?

The engineering concept of load testing is common. If engineers are building a bridge that must carry

50 tons then they test it for 100. Athletes use this concept all the time in preparation for competition. If they must move a 300-pound lineman then they practice pushing a 500-pound sled. If they must run five miles in competition then they regularly train by running ten. Testing in this sense is used to determine integrity, weakness and to improve the opportunity for success.

The theological concept of being tested is about evaluating and strengthening our faith, not about passing or failing. I see many Christian clients who get fixated on determining where the trials and tests in their lives are coming from. They want to know if God is trying to teach them a lesson or if Satan is just tempting them. It really does not matter one way or the other, the important thing is what they do or what they learn. Their problem is that they have a negative view of being tested. James is able to call all things joy because no matter what comes (or who brought it) he has the opportunity to glorify God in it (James 1:2).

As Christians we are called to testify, which means proving our faith not only with our words but also our actions. Athletes who perform spiritually know that testing is about building integrity and strengthening their faith. Testing is a good thing, *"Examine yourselves to see whether you are in the faith; test yourselves. Do you not realize that Christ Jesus is in you – unless, of course, you fail the test"* (2 Corinthians 13:5) (NIV)? Christian athletes want to know where they falter and where they are spiritually vulnerable. Their goal is to be all they can be for Christ and being tested provides them with the feedback that they not only need, but also desire. In this sense, to be tested is the path to self-actualization.

CHAPTER 11

Confession –
Self-Awareness

Spiritually, it is best to start the day with the realization that without God we are limited in what we know, or can do. This is not a defeatist attitude or a low self-esteem statement. It is just being honest about our human condition.

Confession is one of the most important, yet misunderstood, concepts in theology. We said in Chapter 2 that confession is important theologically because it is the first step in the salvation process. This process is confession, justification and sanctification. Confession is important for salvation because it is our part in the process. Without our voluntary movement toward God, salvation cannot be realized.

It is not enough that we move toward God, we must move toward him honestly. This means we have to be aware, open and realistic about who we are and what we believe. Once we are honest with ourselves we begin to see the need for God's forgiveness. We then move toward God on our own, not because we are told to, but because we desire to be complete.

Self-awareness is important for athletes. They need to be realistic about their athletic expectations and goals; they need to be honest about their commitment and desire. For me to say that I love God and deny my sinfulness is like me saying that I'm going to play on the PGA Tour — saying it does not make it so. We cannot expect God to respond to confession based on words without conviction and athletes cannot expect to excel without total commitment. God and coaches have little tolerance for "posers."

In the previous chapter we talked about how many Christians viewed the word "test" as being negative. Unfortunately the word "confession" suffers the same fate. Somewhere along the line Christians began to see confession strictly as penitence, remorse or an act of contrition. They likened theological confession to pleading guilty in court or "coming clean" to their parents. Confession was something you had to do when you were caught doing something wrong. In all of these cases confession is being defined too narrowly.

For example let us look at Joshua 7:19, "*And Joshua said unto Achan, My son, give, I pray thee, glory to Jehovah, the God of Israel, and make confession unto him; and tell me now what thou hast done; hide it not from me*" (ASV). In this verse the word confession seems to track with the negative connotations that most hold. Interestingly enough the word for confession in this verse is the Hebrew word towdah, which means: *an extension of the hand, i.e. (by implication) an open declaration of adoration; specifically, a choir of worshippers.* It is not a negative word at all.

We are also told to confess in Matthew 14:11, "*For it is written, As I live, saith the Lord, to me every knee shall bow, and every tongue shall confess to God*" (ASV). Once again the word for confession means more than once thought. The Greek word for confess here is exomologeo, which is translated: *to agree with, acknowledgment; {con or pro) fess; give thanks; praise.* In my personal Biblical exegesis I find that the word confession refers most often to a call for profession of faith rather than a plea of contrition. I am not saying that word confession never means "confession" as we know it; I am just saying that there are more positive words in its definition than negative. In any case, it is a word that we as Christians need to understand.

As we have said, confession is a key part of the salvation process because it signifies our movement toward God. It is also important because within confession we find two ingredients that are paramount to our relationship with God. The first is *humility*, and the second is, to *trust* God. The first requires us to accept our sinfulness and the second requires that we have faith that God loves us in spite of this sinfulness.

For confession to be profession we need to be humble. We need to know our limitations, the attitudes of our hearts and our sinful nature. We need to need God. Being realistic and honest about our brokenness prevents self-righteousness. For many individuals the idea of focusing on their limitations is viewed as being negative. Their philosophy in life is based on "I can do anything I put my mind to." There is always the danger that success in this life will go to our heads, and spiritually, harden our hearts.

The bottom line is that we may be able to run a multi-million dollar company or hit a baseball 500-feet but we cannot save our own souls. 1 Corinthians 15:50 tells us, *"I declare to you, brothers and sisters, that flesh and blood cannot inherit the kingdom of God, nor does the perishable inherit the imperishable"* (NIV). This verse conveys that when it comes to earning our own salvation, we are very limited. Humility in the New Testament refers to our acknowledgement that "God is great," not that we are weak.

For Christian athletes there is confidence in humility. By placing themselves at the feet of Christ they are assured of God's love, protection and power. Through confession they receive forgiveness and the Holy Spirit. They no longer solely rely on themselves for strength; they can perform with confidence that comes from God.

There is a big difference between arrogance and confidence. Arrogance is defined as: *an attitude of superiority manifested in an overbearing manner based on presumptions, claims or assumptions.* Confidence is defined as: *1 a: a feeling or consciousness of one's powers or of reliance on one's circumstances b: faith or belief that one will act in a right, proper, or effective way.*

Some athletes might say that there is a fine line between being confident and being arrogant. But if you look closely at the definitions of these two words they are significantly different. Arrogance focuses on the individual's superiority and is based solely on predictions and assumptions. Confidence comes from faith and belief in one's ability to perform effectively and appropriately. Confidence is based on fact (actual performance) and is not related to the value of others.

If you compare these two words theologically their differences are even greater. Arrogance is self-centered and boastful; it glorifies the individual at the expense of others. 1 Samuel 2:3, warns the Christian athlete about such an attitude, *"Do not keep talking so proudly or let your mouth speak such arrogance, for the LORD is a God who knows, and by him deeds are weighed"* (NIV). Arrogance comes from our fallen nature, from the flesh,

> *"What comes out of you is what defiles you. For from within, out of your hearts, come evil thoughts, sexual immorality, theft, murder, adultery, greed, malice,*

153

deceit, lewdness, envy, slander, arrogance and folly. All these evils come from inside and defile you" (Mark 7:20-33) (ASV).

As we see from this passage, arrogance is listed with behaviors and attitudes that are carnal and self-centered by nature. You may be surprised to see arrogance in the same list as murder and adultery. Surely arrogance is not as bad as theft or lewdness? Spiritually, arrogance makes this list because it puts the individual's needs above God's. Arrogance, like all things on the list, limits and damages our relationship with him.

Confidence is related to self-esteem. It is not a stretch to say that athletes who compete with confidence have a strong self-esteem. It does not work the other way around. Athletes, who question their personal value, will struggle with self-confidence. In life, and especially in athletics, success is hard to build on the sandy foundation of self-doubt. Plainly stated, self-confidence is built on a good self-esteem.

I often tell my clients that the term "low-self esteem Christian" is a contradiction in terms. As Christians we have value, not from what we have accomplished or deserve, but because God loves us and values us. As a PGA player, Larry Mize was struggling on tour after he had won the Masters. He called Larry Moody who leads a tour Bible study. Mize relates what Moody told him:

"Your sense of identity doesn't come from what you've accomplished or what you

> *do. It comes from knowing you're a child of God. What makes you significant is Jesus Christ. Because you've placed your trust in Him, you're a child of the King, and you're worth the death, burial, and resurrection of Jesus Christ. He put a price tag on you that makes you significant no matter what the world says—no matter how good or bad you play."*

The theologically-based athlete is assured of his or her value and can then perform with a confidence based on this value. Armed with God's blessing and his gifts, the Christian athlete is free to perform without doubt or fear of failure. The foundation of self-confidence for the Christian athlete comes from Romans 8:31, which says, "... *If God is for us, who is against us?*" (ASV).

Spiritually, it is best to start the day with the realization that without God we are limited in what we know, or can do. This is not a defeatist attitude or a low self-esteem statement. It is just being honest about our human condition. Proverbs 3:5 say, "*Trust in the LORD with all your heart and lean not on your own understanding*" (NIV). Accepting our limitations encourages us to put our trust in God and not in ourselves. This is the foundation upon which confession and confidence is built.

Confession requires us to be honest when it comes to the attitudes of the heart. Paul talks about the relationship between God's word and what is in our hearts in Hebrews 4:12, *"For the word of God is alive and active. Sharper than any double-edged sword, it penetrates even to dividing soul and spirit, joints and marrow; it judges the thoughts and attitudes of the heart"* (NIV). Confession ties together what we *say* we believe and what we really *do* believe, *"If you declare with your mouth, "Jesus is Lord," and believe in your heart that God raised him from the dead, you will be saved"* (Romans 10:9) (NIV).

To confess with our words that we love God and feel contempt or bitterness in our hearts is not being honest with God or us. This lack of consistency between what we say and do is addressed in Romans 2:21,*"You, who teach others, do you not teach yourself? You who preach against stealing, do you steal"*(NIV)? To profess our faith we need to have both the words and conviction.

Athletes who talk about the "love for the game" and play for the money or fame are not being forthright. Athletes who talk about the importance of the team and spend most of their time thinking about personal stats and publicity are in denial or are bald-faced lying. We have all heard someone say about an athlete "their heart was just not in it." Anyone who does not think that performance requires heart has never competed. The attitude of the heart tells us more about an athlete than the words that come out of his or her mouth.

Christian athletes struggle less with this inconsistency between what they say and how they feel because they start with a humble heart. They put their heart in performance because God blessed them with the ability and called them to glorify him with this ability, *"Whatever you do, work at it with all your heart, as working for the Lord, not for human masters*" (Colossians 3:23) (NIV).

Confession requires that we understand and claim our sinful nature. We cannot move toward God with honesty without owning the fact that we are all sinners and fall short of the Glory of God. Confession puts God first and lets him know that we are only acceptable in his sight through the sacrifice of Christ,

> " *For what the law was powerless to do because it was weakened by the sinful nature, God did by sending his own Son in the likeness of sinful humanity to be a sin offering. And so he condemned sin in human flesh.*" *(Romans 8:3)(NIV)*

Confession is as much about solidifying our relationship with God as it is about asking for forgiveness. If we see confession as simply "fessing up" to what we think God does not like, then we are missing the fullness of this concept. Confession is understanding and acknowledging our humanness, our need and desire for God's love and guidance. We do not confess to impress — we confess to profess.

Confession demonstrates that we *trust* God. No matter if you define confession as "con or pro fession" the result is the same — *it glorifies God*. Confession is the verbal confirmation of our sinful nature and repenting heart. In Romans 10:10 we are told, "*for with the heart man believeth unto righteousness; and with the mouth confession is made unto salvation*" (ASV). When we confess we are putting words to the attitude of our heart, we are telling God that we acknowledge him as Lord and value this relationship. Confession is a demonstration of our trust and respect. The power in confession is the demonstration of our devotion not just in what we are specifically confessing. In this sense confession is always profession.

God wants us to come to him. The best way to understand confession is to use the example of being a parent. As parents we want our children to come to us with their concerns and problems. We want them to be honest with us no matter what they have done. We do not desire this so we can punish them; we love them and want them to come to us for help. When our children are open and honest with us; it honors us. For them to confess to us professes their respect and love for us. This is the double meaning of confession.

As a marriage counselor I can say with conviction that honesty and trust are at the foundation of a strong relationship. To say that we love someone does not mean much without actions that demonstrate this love. To communicate our love in the midst of vulnerability requires that we be honest and trust others. It tells the other person that they are more important than our own comfort.

Being open and honest with another communicates that we trust them and accept that their words and motives are based on their love for us. In this sense, when it comes to our relationship with God, honesty and trust are at the core of confession. Long time PGA player Hal Sutton describes his relationship with God this way,

"In his Word God tells me that I am adopted into the family of God. I now understand how very special and permanent that is. I love my four children so much, and to think that God loves me even more than I love my daughters and son...It's amazing!"

Christian athletes can take great comfort in the fact that there is someone who knows what they are going through. They know that someone is always there: to hear their fears, frustrations and feelings, to share their hopes and dreams, to know a friend that is concerned and interested in their circumstances and thoughts. They have a father figure who loves, supports and encourages them with unconditional love no matter how they perform. The Christian athlete knows that this person is God and their gratitude is the basis of confession.

CHAPTER 12

Victory – Winning

We live in a "win or lose" culture — it is all or nothing. It appears to me that this is a pretty limited definition of winning. In this sense there are very few winners and a whole bunch of losers, very little success and a lot of failure.

The goal of any athlete is to win. In athletics winning is everything. John Madden once said, "The only yardstick for success our society has is being a champion. No one remembers anything else." Paul (Bear) Bryant has been quoted as saying, "Winning isn't everything, but it beats anything that comes in second." We all of have heard, and probably agree, that "nobody remembers who came in second." Every kid on the playground fantasizes about making the shot at the buzzer to win the big game; they don't dream of missing the shot or coming in second.

Early in the process of writing this book I had a sports agent read some of what I had written. Quite frankly, their response was not positive. The biggest point of contention to what I had written was in reference to winning. She told me that in her experience being a Christian had no bearing on an individual's ability to be successful. She had represented Christian clients that had done everything that a Christian should do and were not successful. These particular athletes prayed, lived a clean life and gave God the glory for all they did. Many of these athletes failed to make it to "the top." They were not immune from getting hurt or cut even when they did reach the top. In this agent's view there is no advantage in sports theology because it "does not pay off when it counts."

The more I thought about this agent's response the more I realized how important the concept of sports theology really is. This particular agent's view is indicative of the limitation of human thinking, which attempts to evaluate spiritual things in worldly terms — to take the big picture and make it small. The problem comes from us defining what success or winning means and then holding God accountable to our definition. This is backwards.

The problem is that in this country we believe that you can only be winner if you come in first. We live in a "win or lose" culture — it is all or nothing. It appears to me that this is a pretty limited definition of winning. In this sense there are very few winners and a whole bunch of losers, very little success and a lot of failure. Once again, in man's infinite wisdom, we have taken a theological truth and squeezed the life out of it. We have taken something that God has already given us, which is eternal, watered it down and made it temporal. We have taken *victory* and turned it into *winning*.

The Psalmist says, "Now this I know: The Lord gives victory to his anointed. He answers him from his heavenly sanctuary with the victorious power of his right hand" (Psalms 20:6)(NIV). As followers of Christ we are victorious. There is no coming in second or losing. God is competitive and constantly competes for our salvation, and it goes without saying, that he plays to win. Once again, limited by our human perspective, we forget that the real game is being played at a higher level and with much more at stake.

In the preceding pages we have talked about how living our lives based on the principles of Christ can change our perspective. By viewing life from God's eyes we begin to see that things are not always what they seem and we can be more than we thought. Being transformed into spiritual individuals provides us access to the knowledge and power of Christ, which brings with it understanding and purpose — we are changed and see things differently. Nowhere is this more evident than when we talk about the concept of "winning."

I have said throughout this book that sports theology is about using the gifts that God has given us. Glorifying God comes from the acknowledgment and development of these gifts to serve him and others. As Christians, success and winning cannot be defined without the glorification of God in it. In this sense, championships may be won and an athlete may reach every goal set in the world of sports, but without Christ at the center of their life, true success is not achieved.

Sports theology has no problem with championships, titles or being at the top of one's profession. A matter of fact, the whole point of sports theology is to allow individuals to perform to their maximum potential. Sports theology attempts to help the athlete compete with the joy and peace that comes from his or her spiritual perspective. To free themselves from the distractions that come from living in the world,

> *"Therefore, since we are surrounded by such a huge crowd of witnesses to the life of faith, let us strip off every weight that slows us down, especially the sin that so easily hinders our progress. And let us run with endurance the race that God has set before us. We do this by keeping our eyes on Jesus, on whom our faith depends from start to finish" (Hebrews 12:1-2) (NLT).*

All athletes compete to win, Christian athletes always do. Christian athletes always win because they have a different definition of winning. They compete (run the race) because God has given them the ability to do so. They train and perform because they have been blessed and called to glorify him through performing. Winning for the Christian athlete in not about coming in first but rather is about competing as a representative of Christ,

> *"However, I consider my life worth nothing to me; my only aim is to finish the race and complete the task the Lord Jesus has given me – the task of testifying to the good news of God's grace." (Acts 20:24)(NIV)*

No matter where the Christian athlete finishes they can glorify God, which is where ultimate victory lies. William Shakespeare once said, "Things won are done, joy's soul lies in the doing." Those who believe that real victory is in performance itself, win no matter the outcome

Athletes who do not fear losing have a better chance to perform at their highest potential. Christian athletes do not view losing in competition as having lost anything. They are complete no matter how they compete. Spiritually based athletes understand that they can glorify God in winning or losing. They know that true character is revealed in how one handles losing. They understand that in the hard times faith is strengthened and their testimony shines. I like what Al Gore once said about losing, "No matter how hard the loss, defeat might serve as well as victory to shape the soul and let the glory out."

I thought long and hard about which athlete I was going to use to demonstrate victorious living. I decided to talk about Jimmy Green. You probably have never heard of Jimmy Green. Jimmy is presently the club pro at The Auburn University Club, a country club in Auburn, Alabama. Jimmy was born in Mississippi and grew up in Daphne, Alabama. It became quite evident at an early age that Jimmy was a gifted golfer. He won pretty much every golf tournament he entered as a teenager and was quickly labeled "one of the best golfers to ever come out of the south."

Jimmy received a golf scholarship to Auburn University and continued to impress those around him with his play as one of the all-time best players at Auburn University. His future looked bright. He turned pro in 1992 and enjoyed limited success. He won a couple of times on the Nike Tour but his best finish on the PGA Tour was a tie for fourth at the AT&T Pebble Beach National Pro-Am. Jimmy was used to coming in first; he was not "winning" now.

Jimmy could play (he is tied at 76th in total eagles on the PGA Tour) but he just could not win. He was only exempt on the PGA Tour in 2001 and had to qualify for every other event. In five years on Tour he missed the cut thirteen times by one stroke. Jimmy left the tour to be a club pro in 2005.

Most people in town do not know Jimmy Green's personal golf history. They know Jimmy as a man of faith. They see him as a strong Christian leader in his church, devoted husband and father and a club pro that loves to teach children and teenagers golf, the game he still loves. There is no resentment or bitterness when you talk to Jimmy about golf. There are no "what ifs" or "life is not fair" when he talks about playing professional golf. I asked him why not?

Jimmy told me that he was able to move on because of his faith in God. He was specific about what he meant. Jimmy told me that God's timing is not always ours. He said that he was not mature enough in his faith and golf became the focus of his life instead of Christ. It became all about winning and the pressure to do so. In his view he had begun to play golf for himself and not for God. He knew this because he would shoot 65 in practice rounds and 75 on the first days of competition.

Jimmy is not bitter because he has faith in God's plan for his life. He told me that working with young people gives him the chance to impact kids and he sees this as part of his mission and purpose. For him, his gifts are to be used for God and this is where he is called to be. He said, "We do not always know what God will call us to do but we must be willing to follow this calling wherever it takes us. This is the meaning in telling God 'here am I'."

Jimmy is not discontented, sure he still wants to be on the PGA Tour, but his contentment comes from serving Christ. He is now in the process of preparing to take another shot at getting his PGA card. That may or may not happen and Jimmy will be OK either way. I asked him why he is willing to go down that same hard, stressful road and he told me that he feels that he is now better equipped spiritually. In his words,

> *"I want to be sure that I did not get in the way of what God had originally called me to do. Perhaps the last four years behind this desk was God's way of preparing me for his ultimate calling. God's will is a process, not an event, and I want to always be willing to do what he requires and go where he leads."*

Jimmy Green is an outstanding example of an athlete who understands the concept of sport theology. He understands the difference between winning and living in victory. No matter what happens, Jimmy wins because his goals are set on a higher standard, a standard that says how he lives is more important than how he performs. Jimmy is a winner because he lives his life based on 1 Corinthians 9:23-25,

> *"I do all this to spread the Good News, and in doing so I enjoy its blessings. Remember that in a race everyone runs, but only one person gets the prize. You also must run in such a way that you will win. All athletes practice strict self-control. They do it to win a prize that will fade away, but we do it for an eternal prize."*

Jimmy Green is a good example for all athletes, not because he is famous, rich or has reached the pinnacle of his sport. The power of his story comes from the fact that he has not achieved any of these things. There are literally hundreds of thousands of Jimmy Greens for every Michael Jordan or Tiger Woods. In the case of Jimmy Green we can see how sports theology works. No matter how things work out, or at what level we compete, knowing and serving Christ brings victory. If at the end of the day we can say, "We have fought the good fight, we have finished the race, we have kept the faith." Then we are winners!

Spiritual mindedness changes the way we see things. It helps us redefine our lives. This is certainly true when it comes to the world's definition of winning. In our culture, and especially in sports, winning means coming in first and everything else is failure. The New Testament talks about victory — not winning. As Christians we all have achieved eternal life, which is the ultimate victory over sin and death. Spiritually speaking we have won on a grand scale that overshadows any definition of winning that man has coined. Christian athletes perform knowing that they have already been crowned victorious.

CHAPTER 13

Playing Inside Out

This is why sports theology is so important. It urges athletes to change direction and move back to God and their original state, which is "created in his image." It urges athletes to change their view of themselves, performance and life.

I overheard a couple of guys in the pro shop the other day giving one of their group some grief about buying a new putter. Evidently this guy was notorious for buying a new putter every time his putting got bad. This sounded a little close to home so a few days later I looked around the house to see how many putters I had. I found seven.

I found putters in closets, under the bed, on the floorboard of my truck and one in the garage that I had cut in half to use the grip. Each one brought back memories of the hope and excitement when they were purchased and the disappointment when they were discarded. I had purchased each one full of faith and confidence only to, once again, be jilted by three-putts. I was looking for a "quick fix."

We are all guilty of this from time to time. I have friends that buy a new car every year or always have the latest phone or electronic gadget. We all know people who have to have the best or "get it first." They are never satisfied; they are like sharks that have to continually swim and eat to live. What are they looking for — what are they missing?

I have clients that come to me for marriage counseling who have been unhappy for fifteen years and are looking for someone to fix it. Even though most do not say it, they want me to tell them or give them something to make years of discord go away (and do this in one hour). The same is true when it comes to medication. Many times clients will ask for medication to solve the problems of their lives as if a pill will make them feel better about who they are. Talk about a quick fix!

This need to be validated from something or someone else is the foundation upon which codependency is built. Simply put, in codependency either party feels that they cannot exist without the other, as individuals they are incomplete. Early in my counseling career I talked to a set of parents that had lost their teenage son to suicide. Their son was a honor student, president of the senior class and had just received a full football scholarship to college. The day after his girl friend broke up with him he hanged himself in the backyard. Evidently she was more important to him than she should have been.

This "what have you done lately to earn your value" mentality is certainly alive and well in the world of sports. How many years did Phil Mickelson have to hear the "you have never won a major" statement, as if that was a measure of his ability or value? Questions like, "can you feel good about your career if you do not win a championship?" are indicative of a culture that is focused on external things for value and not on the internal qualities of the individual.

This fantasy that reaching the ultimate prize in sports brings lasting happiness and meaning is a trap. We have already heard from Bernhard Langer (Chapter 7) who said that he was "miserable" after winning the Masters. We have all heard stories of Super Bowl rings being hocked for money to pay debts or support some addiction. I recently watched an interview with Bill Parcells about his move to the Miami Dolphins. The interviewer asked Parcells why Miami thinks he can turn their team around when his last Super Bowl win (one of two he won) was way back in 1990? I guess it is true that in sports you are only as good as your last performance.

The point in all these examples is that true meaning, peace and fulfillment does not come from the world but rather comes from within. Because of our fallen nature we look for, or attempt to earn, something that God has already given us. We, like Adam, find ourselves outside the gates of the garden searching for meaning and purpose, things we were given when God created us. We attempt to feel powerful and valuable by gathering things that eventually rot and decay leaving us where we started — lost and empty. In 1 Samuel 12:21 we are warned, *"Do not turn away after useless idols. They can do you no good, nor can they rescue you, because they are useless"* (NIV). We will never find enough or achieve enough on our own to compare with God's original love and devotion.

This is why sports theology is so important. First of all it allows athletes to see performance for what it really is, it allows them to *play* the game. Not long after the Pittsburgh Pirates won the 1979 World Series, Willie Stargell talked about the game he played so well. *"When you watch kids playing sandlot baseball, you see kids having fun. And that's basically what I think we should be doing as ballplayers. Whenever people talk about baseball, they don't say, 'Work ball.' They say, 'Play ball.'"*

Christian athletes compete, in the game they love, with the jubilation and joy they had as children. The press, the money or the potential fame that comes with big time sports does not distract those who play from a spiritual frame of mind. They play because they are called to use their gifts to glorify God. Their joy in playing comes from following God's will, *"When you obey me, you remain in my love, just as I obey my Father and remain in his love. I have told you this so that you will be filled with my joy. Yes, your joy will be complete"* (John 15:10-11) (NIV).

The second reason sports theology is important is that it urges athletes to change direction and move back to God and their original state, which is "created in his image." It urges athletes to change their view of themselves, performance and life. Sports theology tells them that peace, purpose and power is internal and not found in the world around them, *"This is what the Lord says: "Cursed are those who trust in mortals, who depend on flesh for their strength and whose hearts turn away from the Lord"* (Jeremiah 17:5) (NIV).

As Christians we are complete, we are made by God with the gifts and skills to accomplish his will. The problem is not that we lack what we need; we just do not understand what we have. Christian athletes compete because of the gifts they have been given, not to define who they are, but <u>because</u> of who they are. They do not perform to be complete; they perform because they <u>are</u> complete, *"Let perseverance finish its work so that you may be mature and complete, not lacking anything"* (James 1:4) (NIV).

Sports theology encourages athletes to rely of the promises of Christ on the field of play and in life. Those athletes who allow their hearts to be filled with the love and power of God will accomplish great things, *"I will give you a new heart and put a new spirit in you; I will remove from you your heart of stone and give you a heart of flesh"* (Ezekiel 36:26) (NIV). Athletes who perform for God, with the Holy Spirit in their hearts, are never distracted by the scoreboard or wins and losses. They compete to glorify God who *"performs wonders that cannot be fathomed, miracles that cannot be counted"* (Job 9:10) (NIV). **This is sports theology; this is playing inside out**.